The Wonderful World of Whirligigs & Wind Machines
15 Projects
Alan & Gill Bridgewater

TAB BOOKS

Blue Ridge Summit, PA

We dedicate this book to Glyn and all those other art-crazy weirdos who are into whirligigs, wind machines, and moving toys. It's a mad, mad world of strings, cogs, trip levers, and pulleys—but isn't it exciting!

FIRST EDITION
FIRST PRINTING

Copyright © 1990 by TAB BOOKS
Printed in the United States of America

Library of Congress Cataloging-in-Publication Data

Bridgewater, Alan.
The wonderful world of whirligigs & wind machines : 15 projects /
by Alan & Gill Bridgewater.
p.   cm.
Includes bibliographical references.
ISBN 0-8306-8349-6   ISBN 0-8306-3349-9 (pbk.)
1. Wooden toy making.   2. Whirligigs.   I. Bridgewater, Gill.
II. Title.
TT174.5.W6B744   1990
745.592—dc20   89-77525
                                                   CIP

TAB BOOKS offers software for sale.
For information and a catalog, please contact:

TAB Software Department
Blue Ridge Summit, PA 17294-0850.

Questions regarding the content of this book
should be addressed to:

Reader Inquiry Branch
TAB BOOKS
Blue Ridge Summit, PA 17294-0214

Book Editor: Cherie R. Blazer
Production: Katherine Brown
Book Design: Jaclyn J. Boone

Contents

Introduction iv

Project 1 • New England soldier whirligig   1
Project 2 • Paddle-arm Quaker whirligig   12
Project 3 • Yankee Army signalman whirligig   25
Project 4 • Drum-beating windmill   38
Project 5 • Tubular bells windmill   51
Project 6 • Clown on an English penny-farthing bike windmill   63
Project 7 • Dutch windmill weathervane   75
Project 8 • Man starting automobile windmill   86
Project 9 • Mad manikins pop-up windmill   100
Project 10 • Tinkle-turn dovecote windmill   115
Project 11 • Pecking bird whirligig   127
Project 12 • Merry-go-round windmill   139
Project 13 • Fisherman windmill   152
Project 14 • Spooky Indian vibrating windmill   165
Project 15 • American Indian in a canoe whirligig   178

Glossary 188

Index 197

Introduction

Welcome to *The Wonderful World of Whirligigs & Wind Machines*! Welcome to a world of sails, propellers, cams, trip levers, drive shafts, pivot joints, working models, and movements. Welcome to a folk art world of woodworked, wind-driven automata: New England soldiers that whirl and twirl, paddle-arm Quakers that flail round in the wind, tubular bells that tinkle, and little mad-manikin figures that bob up and down. The warm touch of a trusted hand tool, the sweet smell of sawdust, and the juicy flow of paints and varnish—*The Wonderful World of Whirligigs & Wind Machines* is all of these and much more.

When we saw our first whirligigs we were amazed and puzzled—little dolls that danced in the wind, Pinnochio type figures with whirling arms, and all manner of woodworked, wind-driven parts that moved, sang, hummed, banged, whistled, and pirouetted when the wind blew life into them.

What fun! What excitement! But where did they come from? How were they made? When were they made? How did they work? And most important of all, could we make them?

Fig. I-1. Late fifteenth century book illustration. Note that the children are playing with windmill toys.

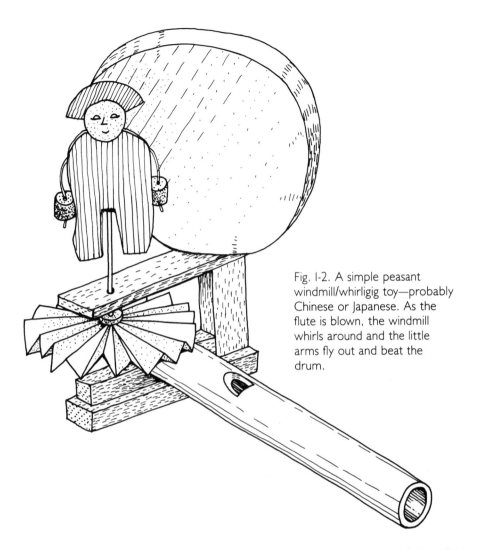

Fig. I-2. A simple peasant windmill/whirligig toy—probably Chinese or Japanese. As the flute is blown, the windmill whirls around and the little arms fly out and beat the drum.

Thus began our long quest into the origins of these uniquely beautiful works of folk art. Inspired by the animated oddities, we delved long and deep. By way of museums, old books and engravings, folk art gallerys, toy shops, travel, and talks with interested parties, we gradually found out what little there is to know about these strange works of art.

Whirligigs and *wind machines* are woodworked, wind-driven sculptures—a curious hybrid of windmills and weathervanes. Made of wood and variously carved, turned, and painted, the moving, puppetlike figures—soldiers with flags, Indians with paddles, etc.—draw life from the wind. On windless days whirligigs are no more than interesting tableau vivant—but, oh my—on windy days when the sails and propellers are being blown around, the figures spring into life and are frenzied and frantic in their dizzy, dancing activities.

If old accounts are anything to go by, whirligigs and wind automata must have once been relatively common sights. Mounted on rooftops and poles, dancing on

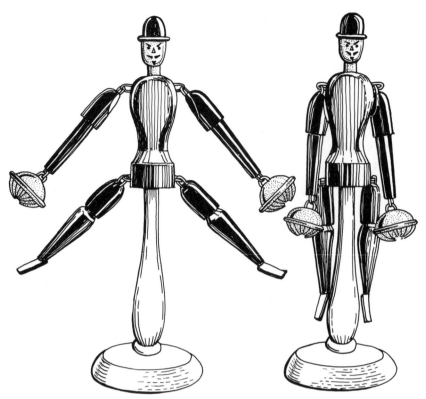

Fig. I-3. A whirligig from a Sonneberg toy sample book (Germany, 1840). As the little figure spins around, the arms flail out and the bells ring.

masts and shop signs, their turning and spinning antics must have gladdened the eye and lightened the heart. But why were they originally built? Were they toys or—like painted hex signs and door carvings—were they used to fend off the devil and protect against the evil eye? In fact, no one really knows. Whirligigs did exist in America from early pioneer days, and old accounts suggest that wind-operated automata were being made in Europe as far back as medieval times. In America at least (especially in coastal districts), whirligigs have long been used as wind speed and direction indicators. In nineteenth-century England, whirligigs were once a common sight. It is believed that they were made and used as shop signs and large silent Sunday toys, or even as bird scarers.

We personally feel that whirligigs and wind machines first saw the light of day hundreds of years ago in the mountainous wood carving areas of Germany and Switzerland. They have so many characteristics in common with cuckoo clocks, town hall figure clocks, music boxes, moving toys, and marionettes made in these areas that there has to be some connection.

Perhaps whirligigs and wind machines were made for no other reason than that they offered craftsmen the unique challenge of making three-dimensional figures that moved. Woodcarving is one thing, but making figures that have movement is a whole new ball game!

Fig. I-4. A New England weathervane made of wood, dated 1875.

In this book, we will explore and use the skills and techniques involved in woodworking. Each and every project involves rolling up your sleeves and getting down to the exciting and enjoyable tasks of sawing, cutting, screwing, sanding, gluing and painting. No matter what your particular woodworking interests—carving, joinery, wood turning, box making, doll making, whittling or naive painting—whirligigs and wind machines can be shaped to suit your own skill level and tool capability.

As to the projects, you can start with the first one and work through to the last, but because they are not arranged in order of increasing complexity, you can work with any project that takes your fancy. Each project has been designed so that it stands alone. Each project has its own project picture, working drawings, sections, details, and set of step-by-step "hands-on" illustrations.

If you are an experienced woodworker, the projects will present a worthwhile challenge. However, if you are a raw beginner, we guide you every step of the way. We suggest you read over the terms in the glossary before beginning, to acquaint yourself with tools and terms used in the book.

As you work through the book, you will see that, from project to project, we suggest many different techniques, tools, variations, and modifications. This doesn't mean that you have to work every project in a completely different way, only that you should consider the range of tools, materials, and techniques—then go for the approach that best suits your needs.

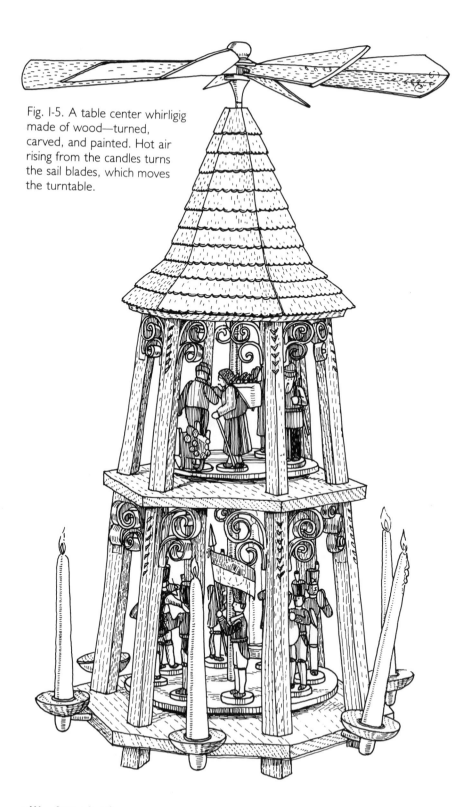

Fig. I-5. A table center whirligig made of wood—turned, carved, and painted. Hot air rising from the candles turns the sail blades, which moves the turntable.

Whirligigs and wind machines are wonderful projects. You will be shaping and painting wood, and building a machine that moves. If you enjoy using your hands—if you are creative—if you want to beautify your home with a museum look-a-like—this is the book for you. Enjoy!

New England soldier whirligig

The New England Soldier whirligig is a classic. With his bright red longtailed coat, splendid moustachios, high boots and plumed hat, he is an upright, fearless, resolute, and heroic man of mettle. Not for this stout-hearted soldier a uniform in disarray or any feelings of indecision; he is an officer and a gentleman (FIG. 1-1).

Inspired by a 22-inch-high soldier whirligig, thought to have been made in New England in the 1850's, this fine fellow is a whirligig in the very best American tradition. Imagine an itinerant wood carver sitting in the shade of a barn with a few simple tools. For a small fee and a meal, the carver—perhaps an old soldier himself—makes the whirligig. Now imagine, mounted high on the barn roof, the finished whirligig turning and spinning in the wind—beautiful!

TOOLS AND MATERIALS

☐ A sheet of good-quality, 1-inch-thick multicore plywood at about 10×18 inches, for the body, arms, and base

☐ A thin sheet of $3/8$-inch-thick white pine at about $6 \times 1^1/2$ inches, for the two paddle blades

☐ Four brass screws about $1^1/4$ inches long, for the base

☐ A 2-inch length of $1/4$-inch diameter brass rod, for the through-body pivot

☐ A 6-inch length of $1/4$-inch diameter steel rod for the figure-to-post pivot

☐ Three brass washers to fit the $1/4$-inch diameter rod

☐ Resin glue   ☐ Acrylic paint, colors to suit   ☐ A pencil and ruler

☐ A large sheet of graph paper   ☐ A bench with a vice

☐ A coping saw or scroll saw

☐ A hand drill with $1/4$-inch and $3/8$-inch bits

☐ A screwdriver   ☐ A square-sided file with a blade no thicker than $1/4$ inch

☐ A knife   ☐ A pack of graded sandpaper   ☐ A selection of paint brushes

DESIGN AND TECHNIQUE

Examine the project picture (FIG. 1-1) and then the working drawings (FIG. 1-2). Of all the whirligigs in the book, this is one of the easiest to make. Note the easy-to-cut, square-edged form; the basic design; and the easy-to-fit construction. The

Fig. 1-1. This traditional American whirligig design with beautifully clean-cut forms was inspired by a museum original dated 1850.

Fig. 1-2. Working drawing and color grid. At a scale of about 2 grid squares to 1 inch, the soldier measures 16 inches high from his toes to the top of his hat. Note the use of 1-inch-thick multicore plywood and the way the paddle blades are set into the arms.

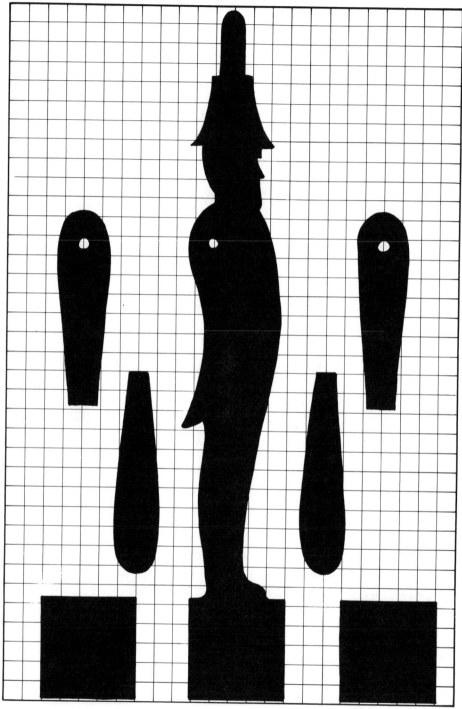

Fig. 1-3. Cutting grid. The scale is 2 grid squares to 1 inch.

paddle blade sails are angled and slotted into the arms. The laminated plywood, three-layer base produces a total wood thickness of 3 inches.

FIRST STEPS

When you have a good understanding of how the whirligig needs to be assembled, draw the design to full size using the cutting plan (FIG. 1-3). Take a tracing, and using the pencil press method, transfer the traced lines through to the working face of the 1-inch-thick plywood. There should be five plywood shapes in all: the main figure, the two base slabs, and the two arms. Label the working face of each arm "outside"—meaning side of the arm that is to be looking away from the figure. Then transfer the traced paddle sails on the white pine.

Now, one piece at a time, secure the wood in the jaws of the vice. Carefully cut out the profiles with the coping saw (FIG. 1-4). When you are sawing, keep the blade at 90° to the working face of the wood and only cut on the waste side of the drawn line. When you have cut out all the forms, take the graded sandpapers and rub the square-cut edges down to a smooth, slightly rounded finish.

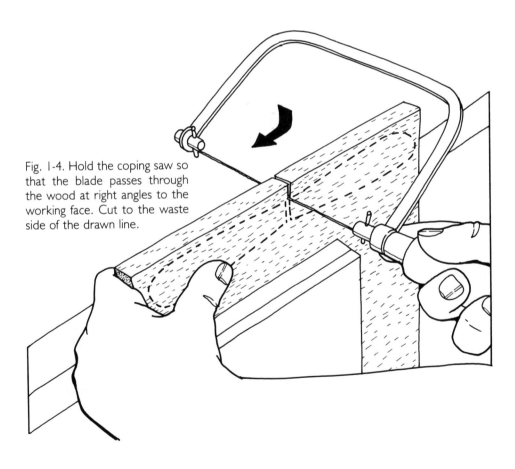

Fig. 1-4. Hold the coping saw so that the blade passes through the wood at right angles to the working face. Cut to the waste side of the drawn line.

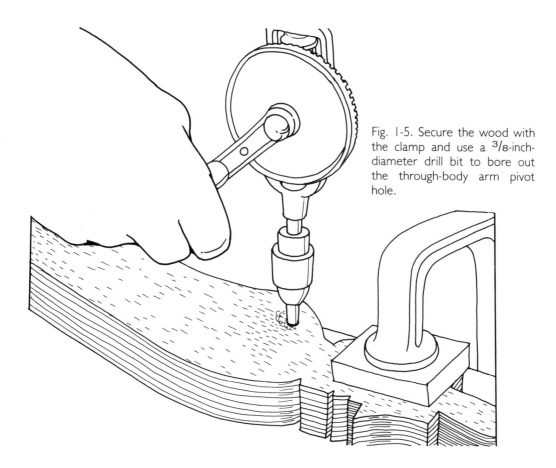

Fig. 1-5. Secure the wood with the clamp and use a ³/₈-inch-diameter drill bit to bore out the through-body arm pivot hole.

Finally, take the drill and bore out the arm pivot holes. Don't forget to clamp a piece of scrap wood on the back to prevent the wood splitting. Make the through-arm holes ¹/₄ inch and the through-body holes slightly larger at ³/₈ inch (FIG. 1-5).

MAKING THE BASE

Take the three main pieces that go to make up the project—the figure and the two base blocks—and try a dry fitting. Sandwich the base of the figure between the blocks so that you have a total wood thickness of about 3 inches, and clamp them up. The base should measure about 3 × 2¹/₂ × 2¹/₂ inches. With the screws well placed so that they don't meet or get in the way of the pivot hole, glue and screw-fix the flanking blocks to the figure (FIG. 1-6).

When the glue is set, secure the figure upsidedown in the vice, and find the center of the base by drawing crossed diagonal lines from corner to corner (FIG. 1-7). Finally, take the drill and the ³/₈-inch drill bit and sink a 3-inch-deep pivot rod hole down into the base.

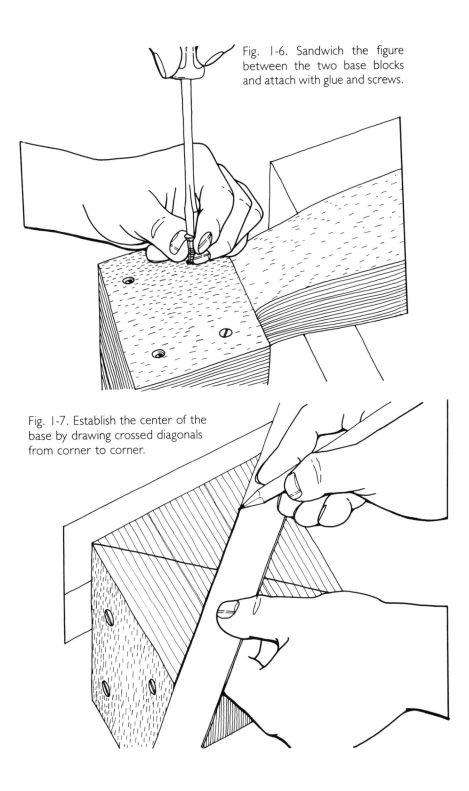

Fig. 1-6. Sandwich the figure between the two base blocks and attach with glue and screws.

Fig. 1-7. Establish the center of the base by drawing crossed diagonals from corner to corner.

MAKING AND FITTING THE PADDLE ARMS

With the knife cut the two paddle blades—the $^3/_8$-inch-thick white pine cutouts—and carve them to a square-shanked, smooth, slightly sharp-edged shape. With the two plywood arms secured in the vice (that is, with the outside faces towards you), mark in the position of the diagonal blade slots using a pencil and ruler (FIG. 1-8).

Aim for slots that are about $^1/_4$ inch wide and 1 inch deep. Use the tenon saw, coping saw, and the file to cut the slots. Saw out a 1-inch-deep U-shaped groove, then use the file to clean up the sides of the slot and take it to finished width. When you fit the blades, adjust the slot and/or the blade until the two pieces of wood fit together. Finally, smear a little glue over mating surfaces and attach the blade with a few small brass pins/oval nails (FIG. 1-9).

PAINTING AND ASSEMBLY

When you have rubbed all the edges and holes down to a smooth finish and you are happy with the overall fit, wipe the entire project with a slightly damp cloth. Arrange a dust-free painting area so that the brushes and paints are at hand. Use a pencil to mark in the boundaries of the large areas of design. Decide how you are going to support the wood while it is being painted: Are you going to hang it from

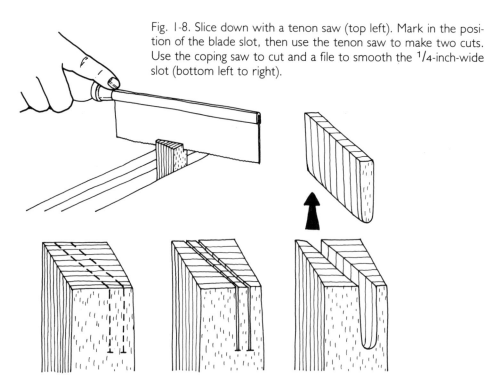

Fig. 1-8. Slice down with a tenon saw (top left). Mark in the position of the blade slot, then use the tenon saw to make two cuts. Use the coping saw to cut and a file to smooth the $^1/_4$-inch-wide slot (bottom left to right).

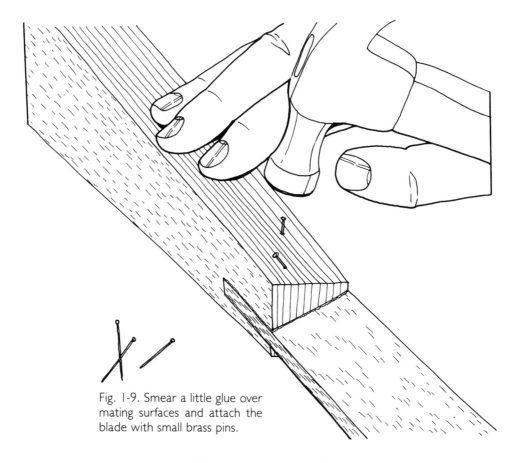

Fig. 1-9. Smear a little glue over mating surfaces and attach the blade with small brass pins.

threads or spike it on wires? Stir and mix the acrylic paints. Remember that the paint needs to dry out between coats.

Now take a brush and lay on the large areas of ground color. You might paint the hat, beard, and boots black; the coat red; the trousers white; and so on. When the ground colors are dry, use a fine-point brush and paint all the small details that go to make up the design: the checkered paddle blades, the eyes, the buttons and the trouser stripes (FIG. 1-10).

After the paint has dried for 24 hours, attach the arms (FIG. 1-11). Push the $1/4$-inch brass rod through the $3/8$-inch-diameter body hole. Slide the washers on the rod, smear the ends of the rod with resin glue, and use a hammer and blocks to fit the arms. When the arms fit tightly on the rod, turn one or the other of them around so that they are set with one up and one down on the same axis.

Finally, bore a $1/4$-inch-diameter hole down into the top of the post. Push the steel rod down into the hole, drop the last brass washer on the rod, and slide the finished whirligig into position onto the rod. Now stand back and admire your work!

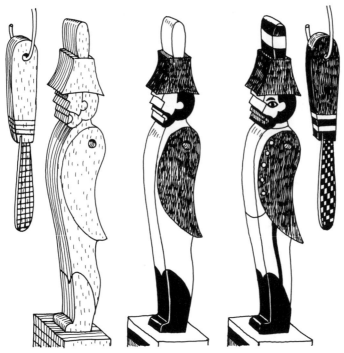

Fig. 1-10. Painting (left to right): Pencil in the main lines of the design, block in the main areas of ground color with a large brush, use a fine-point brush for the small details.

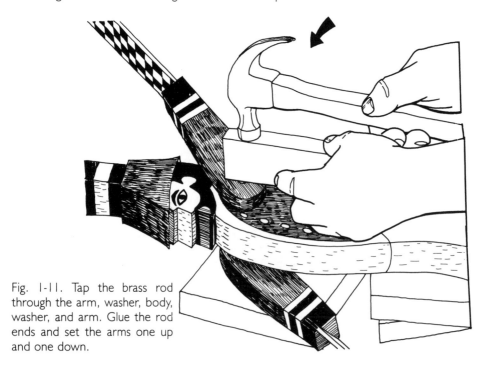

Fig. 1-11. Tap the brass rod through the arm, washer, body, washer, and arm. Glue the rod ends and set the arms one up and one down.

HINTS AND MODIFICATIONS

If you do not have a scroll saw and do not want to saw 1-inch-thick plywood with a coping saw, glue two $1/2$-inch-thick plywood cutouts together.

When working with a coping saw, be sure to have a pack of spare blades handy in case of breakages.

As you set the various shapes out on the plywood, try for spacing that is economical yet practical. You could cut the shapes out in paper and paste them directly onto the wood.

Set the whirligig up out of easy reach. *Note*: When the sails are whirling, they are dangerous.

2
Paddle-arm Quaker whirligig

This whirligig was inspired by a museum original whose description read: "made of wood and metal, 29^1/$_2$ inches high, found in Quakertown, PA, 1875." This is an exciting piece of American folk wood carving. With its square, crude form, simple features, rigid stance, and no-nonsense construction, it is a good example of what has come to be called "folk primitive." This traditional whirligig is a characteristic piece of American whirligig art; it is beautiful! (FIG. 2-1.)

The authentic details—the straight hair, the hat, and so on—are all quite charming. Perhaps the best feature is the way the paddle blade pivot has, quite guilelessly, been made up from a length of plumbing pipe and some salvaged L-bend fittings.

TOOLS AND MATERIALS

☐ A large piece of knot-free, easy-to-carve wood about 8×8 inches square and 36 inches long, for the figure

☐ Two pieces of 4-×-1 wood 24 inches long, for the paddle blades

☐ A 9–10 inch length of galvanized steel plumbing pipe for the through-body pivot, which should have an outside diameter of about 1 inch, and be worked with a male thread at each end

☐ A 6-inch length of galvanized steel plumbing pipe with an inside diameter greater than 1 inch, for the post figure bush

☐ A 8–9 inch length of galvanized steel plumbing pipe with an inside diameter of slightly more than 1 inch, for the through-body bush tube

☐ A 24-inch length of galvanized, 1-inch-diameter steel pipe for the post figure pivot

☐ Three large washers to fit the 1-inch-diameter pipe

☐ Two 90° bends with female threads to fit the 1-inch-diameter pipe

☐ Two 4–5 inch lengths of 1-inch diameter pipe, with male treads to fit the bends

☐ Eight 1-inch screws for the wood-to-metal paddle joints

☐ A large block of plastercine modeling paste

☐ Acrylic paints, colors to suit   ☐ A can of yacht varnish

☐ A large sheet each of graph paper and tracing paper   ☐ A pencil and ruler

☐ A hand drill with a good selection of drill bits

(Continued)

Fig. 2-1. A classic folk-primative whirligig design. Note the wonderful direct style and the easy-to-make paddle arms.

- ☐ A saw tooth drill bit to make a hole for the through-body bush pipe
- ☐ A large coping saw or a small bow saw
- ☐ A hacksaw ☐ A set of woodcarving gouges ☐ A mallet and a hammer
- ☐ A riffler file ☐ A wood rasp ☐ A sharp knife
- ☐ A pack of graded sandpapers ☐ A sturdy workbench with a vice
- ☐ A selection of broad and fine-point paint brushes

DESIGN AND TECHNIQUE

Examine the working drawings (FIGS. 2-2, 2-3, and 2-4). At 8×8 inches square and 36 inches high, this whirligig is one of the largest projects. Note the need for a small working model or *maquette*.

The wood is roughed out with a bow saw, and the form is worked with gouges. As for the pipe fixings—the galvanized pipes used for the through-body arm pivot and the post-figure pivot—you need to use two pipe sizes. One pipe must be able to slide freely within another.

Note the free, uninhibited way in which the whirligig is worked and put together, and decide just how you want your project to be. For example, do you want to simplify the pose and have the legs set together, rather than divided? Or do you want to stay with the same design but have the whirligig much smaller? Consider such points before you start.

MAKING A MODEL AND DRAWING THE DESIGN

When you have a clear picture of how you want to proceed, first make a good working model or maquette using plastercine (FIG. 2-5). Make a rough wooden frame or armature to support the plastercine. Establish the overall pose and final-ize such details as the shape of the face, the set of the features, the costume, the shape of the shoes—everything, in fact, except the paddle arms. This done, use the finished model to help you draw the design out to full size.

Draw out all five views: the figure as seen from top, both sides, the back, and the front. When you are drawing, don't worry too much about the details; con-centrate on the overall large forms in relationship to each other—the size of the head, the width of the shoulders, and the distance from the neck to the coat hem.

When you have achieved the five views, take a tracing. Then use the pencil press tracing method and transfer the lines through to the sides of your chosen piece of wood (FIG. 2-6). Finally, thicken up the main profiles, label the views, and clear the worksurface to begin work.

ROUGHING OUT

With the maquette and the various cutting plan and grid drawings close at hand, mount the wood in the vice so that you can see the side view. Decide how much wood needs to be cut away, then begin cutting with the bow saw. By cutting away small wedges and blocks of wood around the main profile, clear the waste from around the hat, the brow, the nose and chin, and from under the chin and neck, the chest, and the leg and shoes. Work around the figure until you have a profile shape.

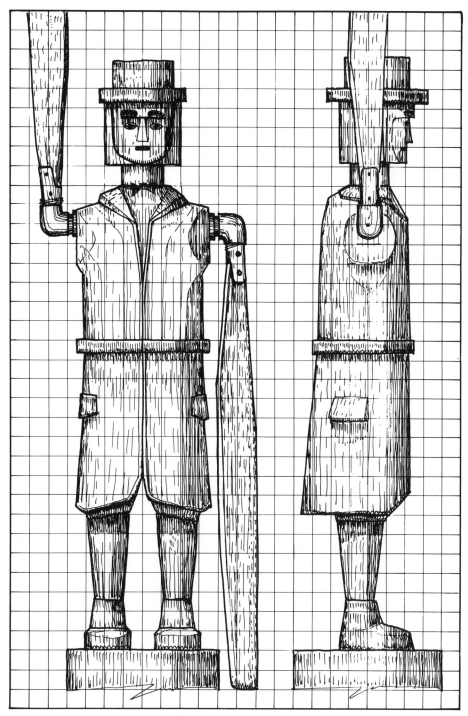

Fig. 2-2. Working drawing. At a grid scale of about 1 grid square to 1 inch, the Quaker figure measures 31 inches high and 12 inches across the paddle-arm shoulders.

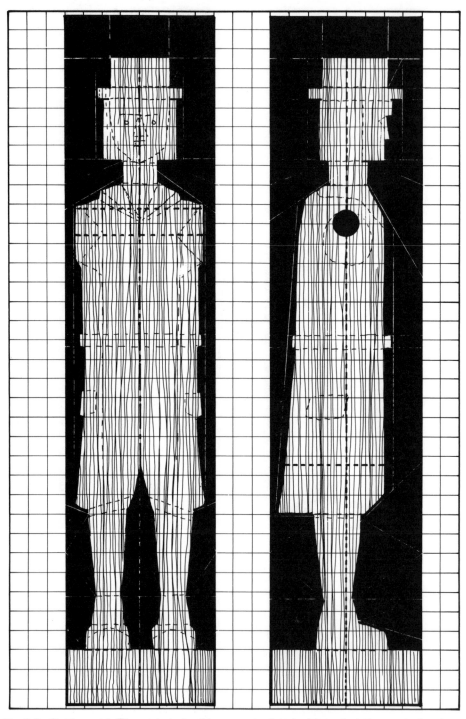

Fig. 2-3. Cutting grid. The scale is 1 grid square to 1 inch. Note that the waste has been squared, triangulated, and cut away.

Fig. 2-4. Working drawing and painting grid. The scale is 1 grid square to 1 1/2 inches. The small pipe detail in the bottom right hand corner is not to scale. Note how the paddle blades are angled so as to catch the wind.

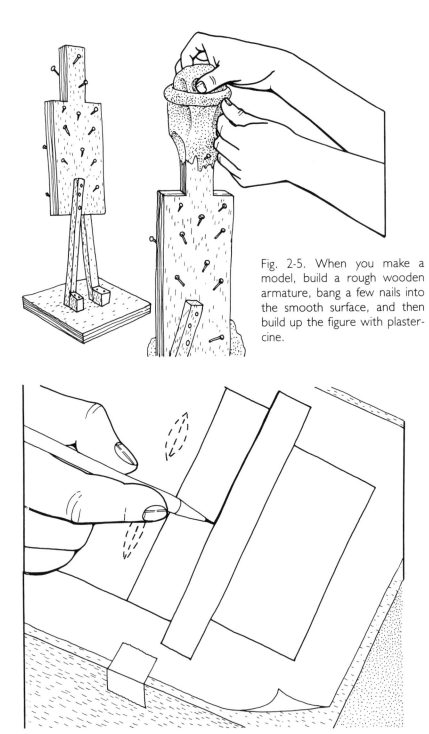

Fig. 2-5. When you make a model, build a rough wooden armature, bang a few nails into the smooth surface, and then build up the figure with plaster-cine.

Fig. 2-6. When you have drawn the design up to full size, take a tracing, and pencil press transfer the traced lines through to your chosen piece of wood.

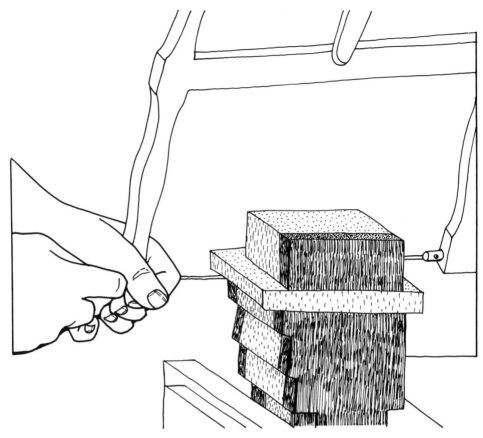

Fig. 2-7. Once you have drawn out the guide lines, clear away the waste from either side of the head. Aim for a clean-cut, stepped profile.

When you have blocked out the side view, reposition the wood in the vice so that you have the front. Redraw the front view of the figure on what is now a stepped face, and crosshatch the wood that needs to be cut away. Now, once again, use the bow saw and cut out wedges and blocks from around the drawn form. Clear away the wood from either side of the hat, from under the hair line and around the neck, from either side of the waist, the sides of the legs, between the legs, and around the base block (FIG. 2-7).

When you have roughed out the front and side views, you will have achieved a squarish blocked-out form. Re-establish the main lines of the figure with a pencil and hatch in the areas that still need to be worked.

MODELING AND CARVING THE FORM

With the wood still mounted in the vise, use the mallet and a small straight gouge, to round up all the rough corners and edges (FIG. 2-8). Don't try to remove the waste wood with great gouge thrusts, but rather work backwards and forwards,

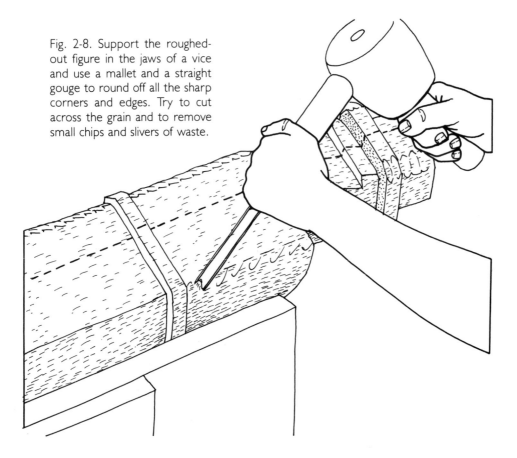

Fig. 2-8. Support the roughed-out figure in the jaws of a vice and use a mallet and a straight gouge to round off all the sharp corners and edges. Try to cut across the grain and to remove small chips and slivers of waste.

over and around the figures. At the same time, scoop out small slivers of waste. You will be getting closer and closer to the desired form. Cut away a piece of waste here and a piece of waste there, referring to the working drawings and the plastercine maquette as you proceed.

Use the tool that you consider best for the job in hand, and cut the angular thrust of the brow, the blunt nose, the jaw, the roundness of hat and hair, the round neck, the coat collar, the belt, the undercutting around the hem of the coat (FIG. 2-9). Don't try, with a wood carving like this, to achieve a realistic roundness. Instead go for a squarish, doll-like look. Cut and work the two paddle blades in like manner: Draw the image out on the wood, cut away the waste with the bow saw, and round the edges with gouge and rasps. Aim for two identical paddles.

FINISHING AND PAINTING

When you have cut and carved the figure, set it upright in the vice and begin finishing it with the knife and sandpaper. Trim the nose; shape the mouth; cut in all the fine details around the hat, collar, pockets and feet; and generally tidy up all the corners and edges. Use the riffler files and craft knife to clean up all the cuts, nooks and crannies (FIG. 2-10).

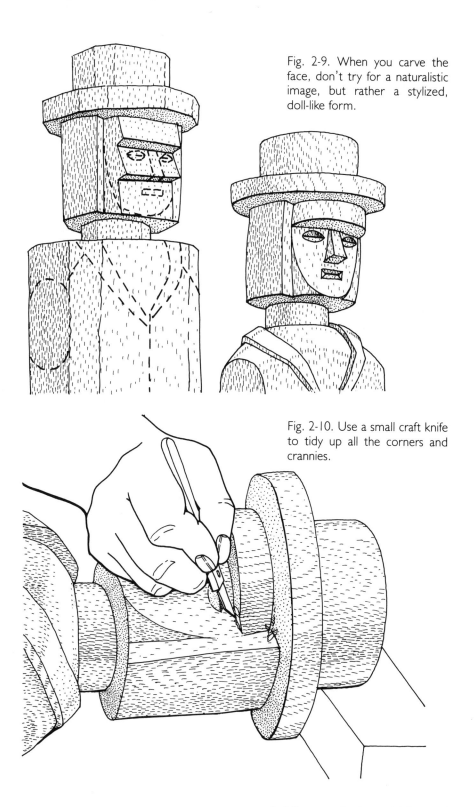

Fig. 2-9. When you carve the face, don't try for a naturalistic image, but rather a stylized, doll-like form.

Fig. 2-10. Use a small craft knife to tidy up all the corners and crannies.

When both the figure and the paddle blades are ready for painting, wipe them over with a slightly damp cloth. Remove all the dust and debris, put away all the tools, clear the bench of clutter, and set out all your paints and brushes. Mix up a range of color *washes* (acrylic paints mixed with water), and use a soft brush to lay on just a hint of color. You might paint the hat and the coat a black/blue, the face a pinky brown, and so on. Try to achieve a finish that looks worn, old, and thin, (refer to FIG. 2-4). Finally, when the paint is dry, cut through the painted surfaces with the finest grade of sandpaper, brush off the dust, and lay on at least two coats of clear varnish.

ASSEMBLY

Start by measuring the diameter of the large outer sleeve pipes. When you have established this diameter and the exact position of the through-body arm pivot, take the drill and bore out a clean, well-placed hole. The arm hole needs to run squarely through the body from shoulder to shoulder. Now tap the 8–9-inch bush pipe gently through the hole. The pipe should stick out about 1/2 inch on

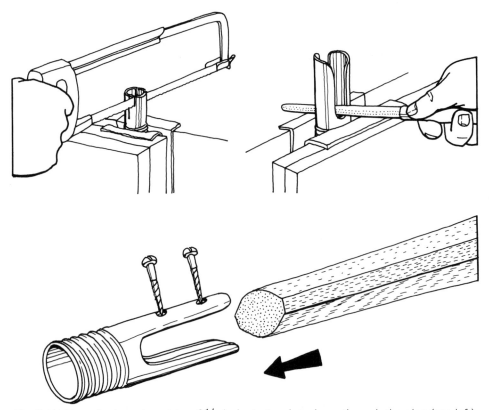

Fig. 2-11. Use a hacksaw to cut two 2¹/₂-inch starter slots down through the pipe (top left). Use a file to remove all the rough edges and burrs (top right). Slide the carved end of the paddle shank into the now pronged tube and attach with round-head screws (bottom).

either side of the body and fit tightly. This done, push the 1-inch-diameter pipe through the larger bush pipe, slide on the washer, and screw on the L-bends. Screw the bends as tightly as possible, and leave them set—one up, one down.

When you fit the short lengths of pipe to the paddle shanks, first examine the working drawings and note how the pipes need to be cut, filed, and drilled. Cut two slots in each pipe and remove the waste with a round file. Aim for a U-shaped slot that is about $2^1/2$ inches long and $^1/2$ inch wide (FIG. 2-11). Work the tube at each side of the U, and modify the paddle shank so that the two-pronged tube slides over and holds the wood. Drill and screw-fix the shanks, smear resin glue over the pipe threads, screw the blades into the pipe bends, and set the angle of the paddle blades.

Finally, bore a hole into the base, tape a short length of 1-inch diameter pipe into the hole, strap the pivot bush shaft onto a post (FIG. 2-12), and place a washer on the pipe. Drop the figure on the shaft, and the whirligig is ready for action.

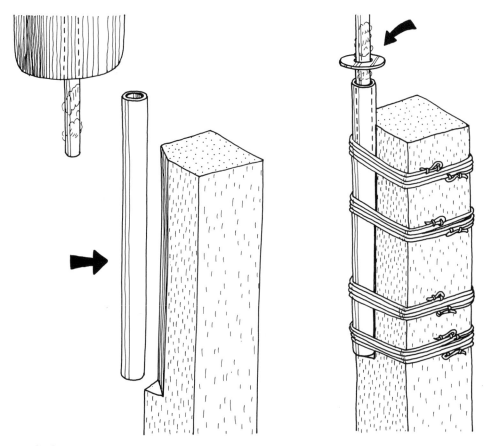

Fig. 2-12. Fixing the whirligig to the mounting post. Tap the 1-inch-diameter pipe into the base of the whirligig. Remove a corner slice from the post and strap the pivot bush in place (left). Place the washer on the pivot pipe and slide the figure into place (right).

Paddle-arm Quaker whirligig   23

HINTS AND MODIFICATIONS

At 8×8 inches square and 36 inches high, this whirligig represents quite a hefty undertaking. If you like the project you can make a smaller whirligig, as long as you modify the various pivots and use slender rods rather than pipes. You could also work it with a knife rather than with gouges.

For smaller whirligigs, use $1/2$-inch-thick multicore plywood for the paddle blades. Make sure that you use an exterior grade. Also, woodcarving can be a bit tricky: Use a good straight-grained, knot-free wood and secure the wood in the vice. Keep your tools sharp.

If the whirligig is going to be set up in an exposed position, it would be a good idea to use through-bolts, rather than screws, to fix the paddle blades to the pipe ends.

3

Yankee Army signalman whirligig

The Army Signalman whirligig is a charmer (FIG. 3-1). Standing about 16 inches high and beautifully decked out in proud U.S. army blue, he was inspired by a whirligig from the Karolik Collection in the Boston Museum of Fine Arts.

The museum whirligig, made in about 1860, is like one that Thomas Hardy describes in his book *The Trumpet Major*:

> It rose from the upper boughs of the tree to about the height of a fisherman's mast, and on the top was a vane in the form of a sailor with his arms stretched out. When the sun shone upon this figure it could be seen that the greater part of his counternance was gone, and the paint washed from his body so far as to reveal that he had been a soldier in red before he became a sailor in blue . . . this revolving piece of statuary could not, however, be relied on as a vane, owing to the neighboring hill, which formed variable currents in the wind.

So there you have it: Although whirligigs are now rare, and although it has been suggested that they were childrens' playthings rather than weather vanes, it seems whirligigs of this character were once commonplace wind speed and direction indicators.

TOOLS AND MATERIALS
- [ ] A piece of $4^1/_2 \times 4^1/_2$-inch-square wood, about 24 inches long, for the main figure. Use a good turning wood such as beech
- [ ] A piece of $1^1/_2$-$\times$-$1^1/_2$-inch-square wood about 8 inches long, for the arms
- [ ] A piece of high-quality, $^1/_4$-inch-thick exterior grade plywood at 2×8 inches, for the arm paddles/sails
- [ ] A piece of $^1/_4$-inch-diameter metal rod (mild steel, aluminum, or brass) about 7 inches long, for the arms/body pivot
- [ ] Cardboard   [ ] Two brass washers to fit the rod

(Continued)

Fig. 3-1. This design was inspired by an American museum whirligig dated 1860. Note the accurate attention to the uniform details.

☐ A piece of $3/8 - 1/2$-inch metal rod about 12 inches long, for the main figure-to-post pivot (with a washer to fit)

☐ Two tube resin glue ☐ A can each of wood primer and undercoat

☐ Enamel gloss paint, colors to suit ☐ A small wood turning lathe

☐ A set of turning gouges, including a skew chisel

☐ A pencil and measure ☐ A pair of scissors ☐ A pair of callipers

☐ A pair of compasses ☐ A plane or drawknife ☐ A small straight saw

☐ A drill with $1/4$-inch, $5/16$-inch, and $5/8$-inch bits

☐ A woodworking bench with a vice ☐ A pack of graded sandpapers

☐ General workshop tools and materials

DESIGN AND TECHNIQUE

Examine the working drawings (FIGS. 3-2, 3-3, and 3-4). Note how the workpiece needs to be turned on the lathe, sawn, and whittled. From top to toe, the figure measures about 16 inches high, and once turned, it needs to be sliced and carved. By carving and whittling, the basic turned shape can easily be transformed into a character figure. The soldier needs to be knifeworked at the back, either side of the arms, and from waist to base to separate and shape the legs and around the brim of the hat. A single turning is split in half to make the two arms. Note the paddle arms, the arms-to-shoulder pivot, and the figure-to-post pivot shaft. Study all the plans, sections, and details until you know exactly how the project needs to be turned, carved, and assembled.

TURNING THE CYLINDER

Start by making sure the lathe is in safe working order. Check the on/off control, see that the tools are arranged and close at hand, make sure that your sleeves are rolled up and your hair is tied back, and so on. In fact, if you are a beginner, read through the lathe manual and through our glossary data. **Note:** It is important that you are familiar with lathe safety precautions. If you have any doubts, contact an experienced woodturner.

Check your $4^1/2$-x-$4^1/2$-inch-square, 24-inch-long piece of wood to make sure it is completely free from flaws like knots, stains, ragged grain, and splits. Then cut the ends of the wood square and find the end centers by drawing diagonals across the $4^1/2$-x-$4^1/2$-inch squares. With the compass set to a radius of $2^1/8$ inches, set each end of the wood out with a $4^1/4$-inch-diameter circle. Mark tangents to the circles. Shade in the resultant octagons and link them by lines drawn along the length of the wood (FIG. 3-5). With the wood set secure in the vice, take the plane and clear away the four areas of corner waste. With the wood now very nearly round, set it securely between lathe centers.

Check that the centers are well into the wood, and set the tool rest so that it is as close as possible to the work and a little below the center line. Switch on the power. With the tool of your choice—you might use a heavy, round-nosed scraper or a deep U-section gouge—work systematically backwards and forwards along the spinning wood, clearing away the rough. Continue until you have worked a smooth $4^1/4$-inch-diameter cylinder.

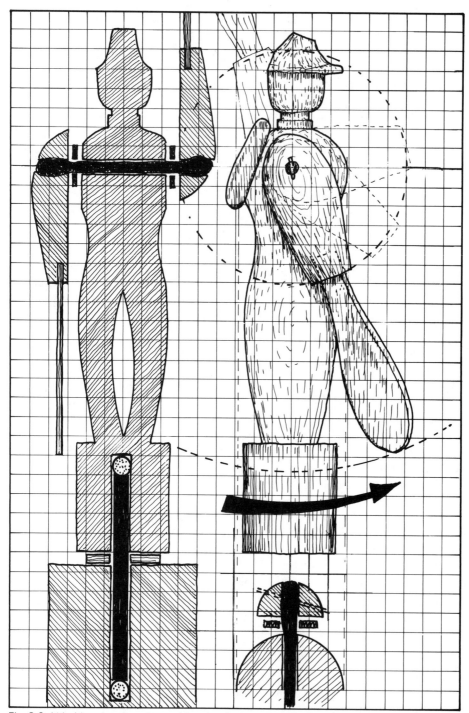

Fig. 3-2. Working drawing. At a grid scale of approximately 3 grid squares to 2 inches, the turned figure stands about 15 – 16 inches from top to toe. Note the split turning for the two arms, the metal through-body pivot, and the efficient rod and ball bearing base pivot.

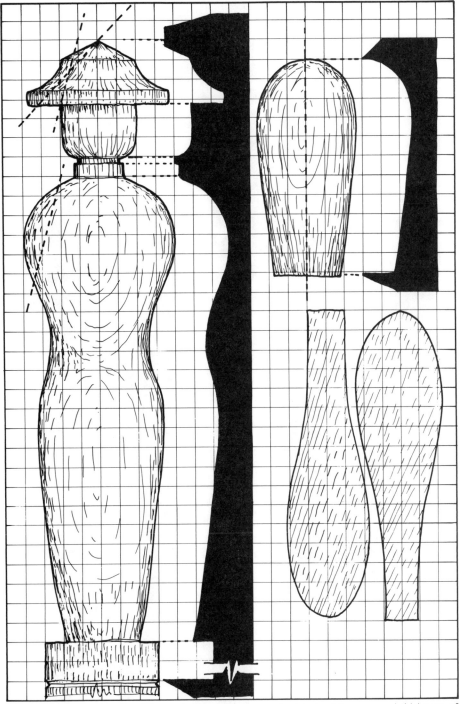

Fig. 3-3. Working drawing. The scale is 2 grid squares to 1 inch. Allow a good thickness of wood at the base. Make two cardboard templates, one for the main body turning and one for the arms. See how the turning needs to be cut and carved.

Fig. 3-4. Painting grid. The scale is 2 grid squares to 1 inch.

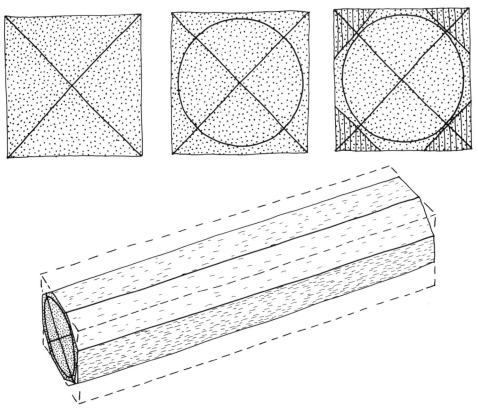

Fig. 3-5. Turning off the basic cylinder. Find the end centers by drawing crossed diagonals. Set each end out with a $4^1/4$-inch diameter circle. Mark tangent lines to the circle and shade in the areas that need to be cut away (top left to right). Link the resultant end-of-wood octagons with lines, and use a plane to clear away the waste (bottom).

TURNING THE BODY AND ARM PROFILES

Make the cardboard template for the main figure and mark the wood out along its length. Allowing for end waste, step off the wood at: the top of the head, the bottom of hat brim, the neck, the collar, the waist, and the toes. With measure, callipers, cardboard template and parting tool ready, switch on the power, and work from mark to mark, cutting in pilot or depth guides. Lower and waste the diameter of the wood at the pilot holes until the sequence of calliper readings checks off against the working drawing.

When you are sure that the work is correct, take the skew chisel and—using the template and the pilot cuts as a guide—work all the humps and hollows that go to make up the design (FIG. 3-6). Don't try to cut away the waste in great deep thrusts, but rather gradually take off the wood, continually running the tool from high to low ground. Work from face to neck, from chest to neck, from chest to waist, from thighs to waist, and so on, while cutting away the waste with little sliding side sweeps. As you get nearer to the form, use more delicate and cautious

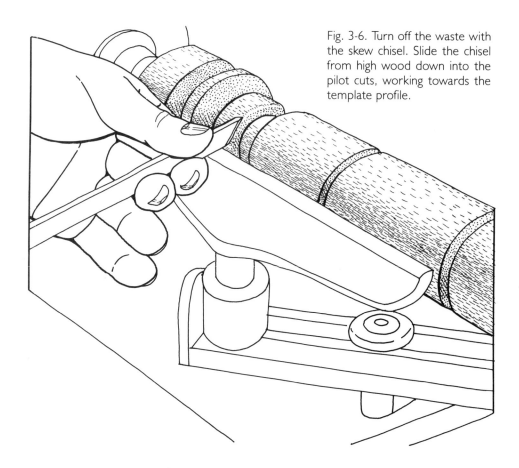

Fig. 3-6. Turn off the waste with the skew chisel. Slide the chisel from high wood down into the pilot cuts, working towards the template profile.

cuts. When you have achieved a good template fit, take the graded sandpapers and work the turning to a smooth finish.

Finally, when you have removed the turning from the lathe, take the 8-inch piece of $1^1/_2$-×-$1^1/_2$-inch-square wood and, with the help of the arm template, work the little fat arm shape in the same way.

CARVING AND WHITTLING

When you have achieved the two basic turnings—the main figure and the skittle shape that makes up the two arms—use the straight saw to cut them down into their component parts. Trim the waste away from the top and bottom of the figure, and cut the arm skittle in half along its length to make the two half-circle, flat-faced arms (FIG. 3-7). This done, examine the working drawing details again, then use your saw to cut away the waste. Remove the wood at: the curve of the back, the arm pivot points, and the brim of the hat at the back and at the sides (FIG. 3-8).

Take care when you are whittling with the knife to remove the wood between the legs and at the turned hat brim. Don't let the knife slip into the fragile short grain. Run your knife backwards and forwards, over and around the turned skittle, until you achieve the desired form.

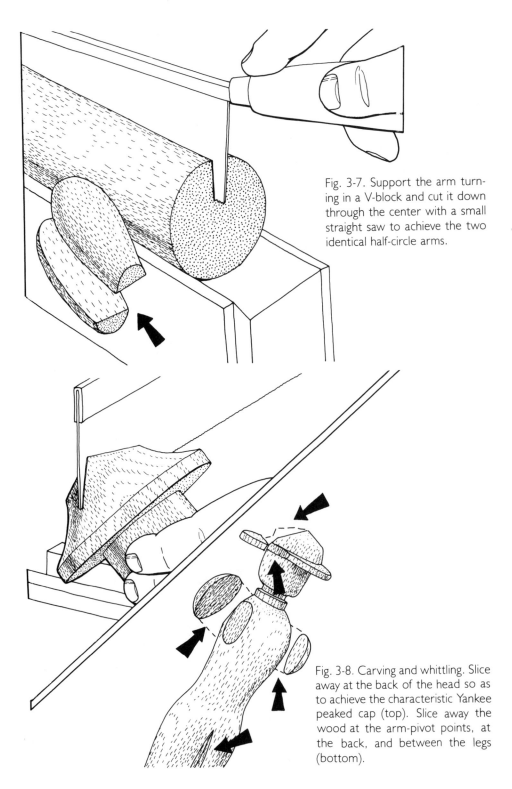

Fig. 3-7. Support the arm turning in a V-block and cut it down through the center with a small straight saw to achieve the two identical half-circle arms.

Fig. 3-8. Carving and whittling. Slice away at the back of the head so as to achieve the characteristic Yankee peaked cap (top). Slice away the wood at the arm-pivot points, at the back, and between the legs (bottom).

FITTING THE PADDLE BLADES AND DRILLING THE ARMS

On the working drawing details, notice how, side-by-side and flat-face down, the two paddle blades seem identical. Note also how the blades are slotted diagonally into the arms. Trace off the paddle blade shape (FIG. 3-3) and transfer the traced lines through to the plywood using the pencil press method. Cut the shapes out with the coping saw and use the graded sandpapers to rub the cut edges down to a smooth finish. One piece at a time, secure the arms in the vice, and use the straight saw and the coping saw to cut out the long paddle slots. Fit and fix the paddles in the slots with glue and small nails or panel pins (FIG. 3-9).

When you have made the three forms—the turned, carved, and whittled figure and the two paddle-blade arms—set them out on the work surface and establish the exact position of the pivotal rod holes. These are the holes through the top of the arms and the hole through the body. When you have checked and double-checked the position of the holes, take the drill and bore them out (FIG. 3-10). Bearing in mind that the 1/4-inch pivotal wire needs to be a tight fit in the arms and a loose fit through the body, use the 1/4-inch bit for the arm holes and a 5/16-inch bit for the body. Then take a small piece of scrap wood and make and attach the little backpack.

Finally, with the figure secured head-side down in the vice, take the 5/8-inch-diameter drill bit and run a hole down into the center of the base.

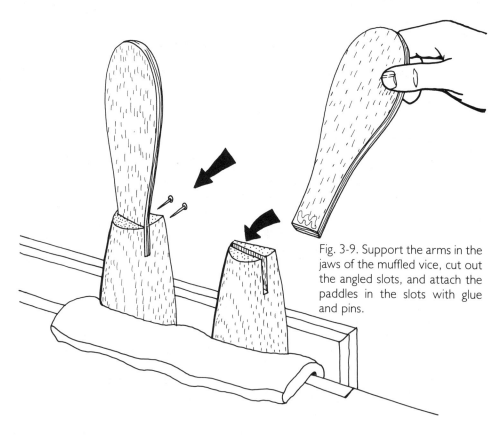

Fig. 3-9. Support the arms in the jaws of the muffled vice, cut out the angled slots, and attach the paddles in the slots with glue and pins.

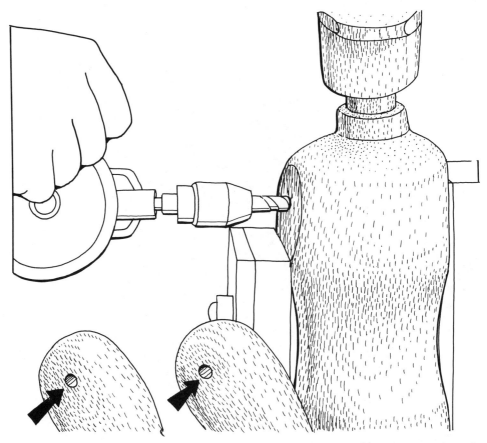

Fig. 3-10. Drill a $5/16$-inch-diameter hole through the body and $1/4$-inch holes through the arms.

PAINTING AND ASSEMBLY

When you have drilled out the various holes, rub the wood down to a good finish, and dust off the piece. Note how the colors need to be worked in relation to each other, and set out your brushes and paint. Remember to let the paint dry out between coats, and lay on a primer, an undercoat, and the top gloss coat. Use a medium-sized brush to paint large areas—the skin and the blue uniform. When the large areas of ground color are dry, use the fine-point brush to pick out all the small details. You might paint the trim on the hat, jacket, and trousers gold, and the hair and eyes black (FIG. 3-11).

When the paint is dry, pass the metal rod through the figure, slide on the two washers, and hammer the ends of the rod until they deform and flatten. Smear a generous amount of resin glue in the arm holes, and—noting that the arms need to be set one up and one down on the same axis—push-fit the arms on the rod (FIG. 3-12). Bore a $5/8$-inch-diameter hole down into the top of the post, to a depth of 6 – 8 inches.

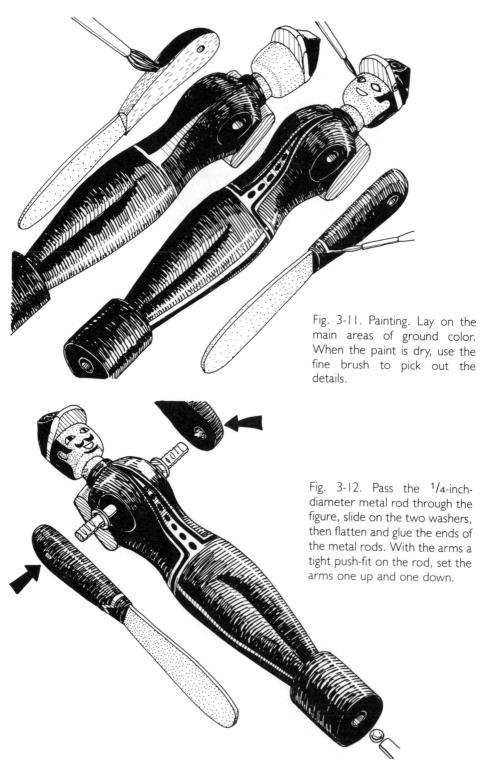

Fig. 3-11. Painting. Lay on the main areas of ground color. When the paint is dry, use the fine brush to pick out the details.

Fig. 3-12. Pass the 1/4-inch-diameter metal rod through the figure, slide on the two washers, then flatten and glue the ends of the metal rods. With the arms a tight push-fit on the rod, set the arms one up and one down.

Finally, pop a ball bearing down into the post hole, grease the rod, and drop it in after the bearing. Place the other ball bearing on top of the rod and drop the finished whirligig in position.

HINTS AND MODIFICATIONS

When you are turning wood, it is most important that you use a suitable, easy-to-turn wood that doesn't have too many grain twists and knots. Beech, apple, ash, lime or holly work well. Buy your wood from a specialist supplier.

When you are working on the lathe, always run through a safety checklist just before you turn on the power: Is the on/off switch working? Is the workpiece securely mounted between centers? Is the tool rest just clear of the wood? Are the tools close at hand but out of harms way? Is the floor around the lathe clean, dry, free from debris? If there is anyone else in the workshop with you, are they standing a safe distance away? Is your hair tied back and your sleeves rolled up? Also, *never* leave a child alone in the room with the lathe.

Some more pointers: When you are whittling and carving, use the knife with a restrained thumb paring action. Use a waterproof resin glue. If you decide to use acrylic paint, protect it with a few coats of yacht varnish.

4
Drum-beating windmill

The drum-beating windmill is a noise-making wind machine in the classic cuckoo clock and music box traditions. It has all the characteristics that we now recognize and describe as Tyrolean, or German fairytale gothic. There are moving parts, pivots, drive shafts, cams, and trip levers, all made of cut and carved wood, and all beautifully assembled (FIG. 4-1).

This type of wind-driven automation is exciting in its inexorable function: the wind drives the sails, the main drive shaft slowly turns, the staggered trip levers around the shaft systematically press down on the drumsticks, and so the drumsticks rise and fall on the drum.

TOOLS AND MATERIALS

- [ ] A sheet of best quality $3/8$-inch-thick multicore plywood, for the box, sails, tail, levers and spacers—a sheet about 24×48 inches should be enough
- [ ] A 12-inch length of 1-inch-diameter broomstick dowel
- [ ] A 16-inch length of 2×1-inch hardwood, for the sail blocks
- [ ] A 16-inch length of $3/4$-inch-diameter dowel, for the two drumsticks
- [ ] A 12-inch length of $3/8$-inch-diameter metal rod, for the drumstick pivot
- [ ] Two brass washers to slide over the $3/8$-inch rod
- [ ] A 7-inch length of metal or plastic tube for the drumstick spacers, that will slide over the $3/8$-inch-diameter metal rod
- [ ] A sheet of stout leather at about 6×10 inches, for the drumskin
- [ ] A handful of brass dome-head tacks/brads to fix the leather
- [ ] A handful each of $3/4$-inch-long brass pins and screws
- [ ] A can of waterproof wood glue
- [ ] A 24-inch length of $1/2$-inch-diameter metal rod, for the main pivot
- [ ] Acrylic paint—colors to suit □ A can of high-gloss yacht varnish
- [ ] A large sheet each of graph paper and tracing paper
- [ ] A pencil and measure □ A try square □ A straight saw
- [ ] A coping saw □ Chisels—$1/4$ inch and $3/4$ inch
- [ ] A brace with bits at 1 inch, $1/2$ inch, and $1/4$ inch
- [ ] A hammer □ A pack of graded sandpapers
- [ ] A selection of paint brushes

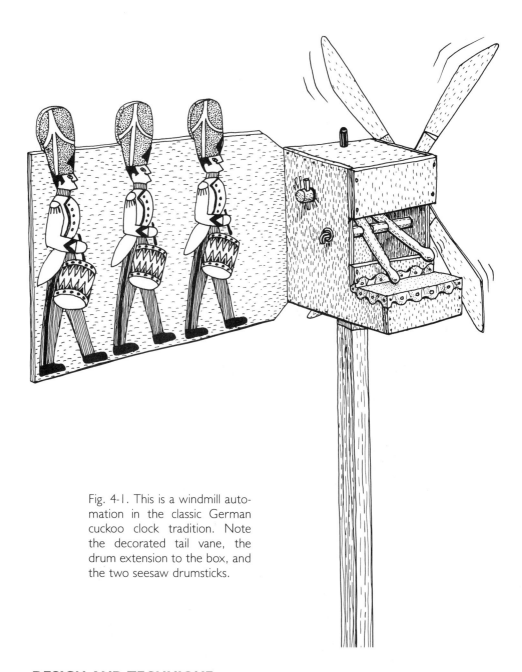

Fig. 4-1. This is a windmill automation in the classic German cuckoo clock tradition. Note the decorated tail vane, the drum extension to the box, and the two seesaw drumsticks.

DESIGN AND TECHNIQUE

Before you buy your materials, study the various working drawings (FIGS. 4-2, 4-3, and 4-4) to see how the machine is made and put together. Note the simple box construction and the way the base and sides of the box extend to form the drum, as well as how the drumsticks are pivoted in a seesaw fashion so that they trip and

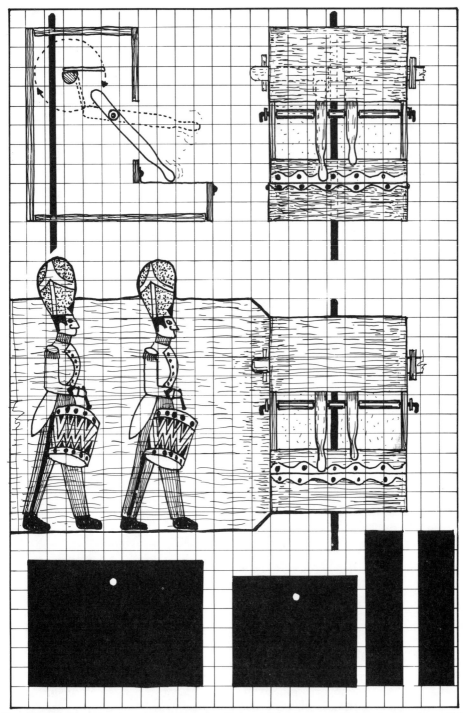

Fig. 4-2. Working drawing. At a grid scale of about 1 grid square to 1 inch, the drumstick movement is contained in a box that measures about $10 \times 10 \times 8$ inches. Note how the driveshaft trip levers need to press down on the drumsticks.

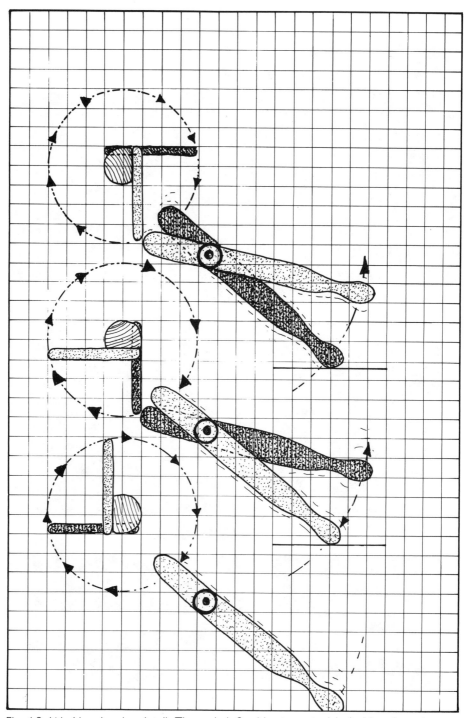

Fig. 4-3. Working drawing detail. The scale is 2 grid squares to 1 inch. Note how the two quarter-set trip levers press down on their drumsticks swiftly, one after the other, to produce a quick double beat with every revolution of the drive shaft.

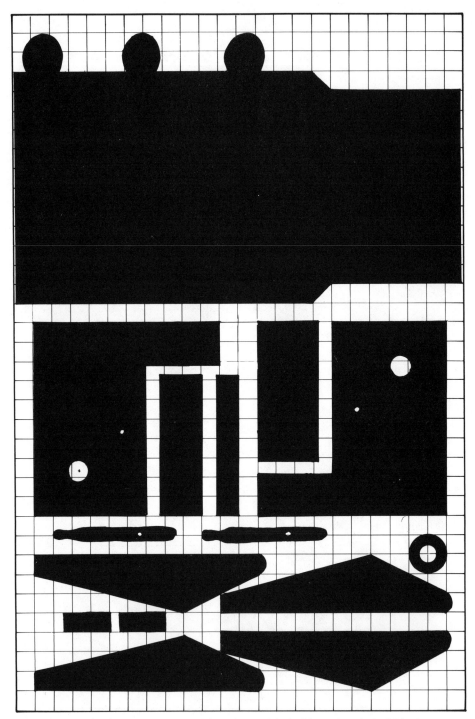

Fig. 4-4. Cutting grid. The scale is 1 grid square to 1 inch. Note that the sail blocks are not shown on this grid.

fall. It is possible, by widening the box, increasing the number of sticks and trip levers, and setting the levers in a spiral formation around the drive shaft, to have the machine play quite complicated drumrolls.

Consider how you might modify the shape, form, and action of the machine. Then sit down with a pencil, ruler, and graph paper and draw the design to full size. If you want to change the design, or if you can't quite see how certain parts need to be fitted, make a full size working prototype out of cardboard.

PREPARING THE WOOD AND FIRST CUTS

When you have drawn the design to full size, trace the flatwood shapes that go to make up the box, then carefully pencil press transfer the traced lines through to the working face of the plywood. Check the size of the shapes with a pencil and ruler, mark in the position of the various holes, and label the forms so that there is no doubt as to their place and function.

Use the straight saw to cut out the eight flat forms that go to make up the box. You should have the main tail vane, the two L-shaped sides, the top and the bottom, the panel that goes above the drumsticks, the narrow strip that goes under the drumstick hole, and the strip that makes up the front of the drum box. Use the brace and bits to work the various holes, then rub all the cut edges down to a smooth finish.

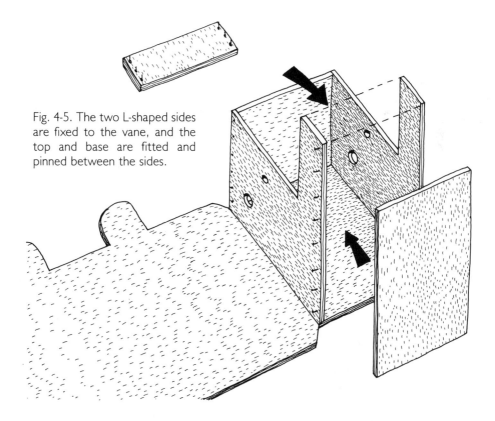

Fig. 4-5. The two L-shaped sides are fixed to the vane, and the top and base are fitted and pinned between the sides.

Use the large tail vane sheet as the base or starter board. Butt, glue, nail, and screw the various pieces edge to edge, so the two L-shaped sides are fixed to the vane and the top is set between the side pieces (FIG. 4-5). When you fit the two front panels, leave out the glue and fix them with screws. Finally, check that the box is square, wipe away extra glue, and put it to one side until the glue has set.

ATTACHING THE MAIN DRIVE SHAFT AND TRIP LEVERS

When the glue has set, place the box vane-side down on the worksurface, remove the two front panels, and make sure that the drive shaft holes are well aligned. Now slide the 1-inch-diameter dowel through the holes and mark on the shaft the position of the two trip levers. Make sure the levers are set sequentially around the shaft at 90° to each other. From left to right along the shaft, the levers need be set at 3 and 6 o'clock (see FIG. 4-3). Mark in the position of the two trip levers, and cut out the seatings with the saw and chisel. One piece at a time, saw down through the dowel thickness to the depth of the trip lever and use the chisel to clear out the waste (FIG. 4-6).

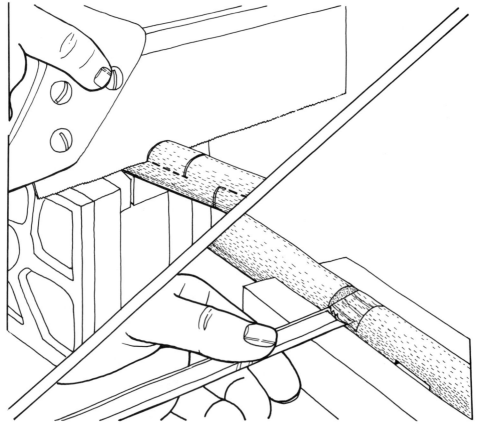

Fig. 4-6. Fitting the trip levers. Saw down into the thickness of the drive shaft to the depth or thickness of the trip lever (top). Use the chisel to clear away the waste; aim for a tight flat-bedded fit (bottom).

When you have the two flat beds or seatings, slide the dowel through the two shaft holes and screw the trip levers into position.

FITTING DRUMSTICKS AND SPACERS

When the trip levers have been screwed down, slide and adjust the shaft within the box so that the levers are set either side of center. Lash the whole drive shaft unit in place with a length of string. Fit and fix the tail end of the shaft with a wedge peg. Now, use the $3/4$-inch-diameter dowel to make the two drumsticks. The sticks need to be about 7 inches long, shaped and rounded, and drilled at a point about 2 inches from the handle end (FIG. 4-7).

Note the various critical measurements: The two levers are about 1 inch apart, the drumsticks are each $3/4$ inch in diameter, and the box is about $6^3/4$ inches wide. Cut the plastic/metal spacer tube into three slightly oversized lengths. Now, at one and the same time, push the $3/8$-inch drumstick rod/wire in through the box and slide the spacers and drumsticks into position (FIG. 4-8).

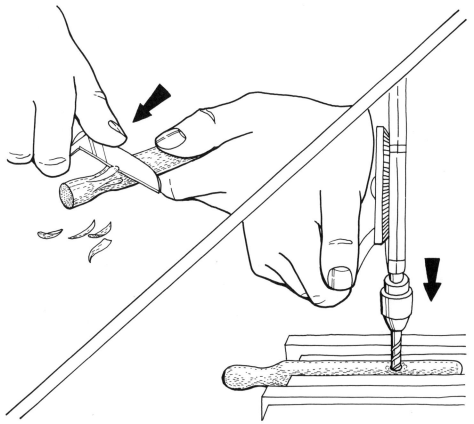

Fig. 4-7. Fitting the drumsticks. At about 7 inches long, shape the ends of the dowel so as to achieve the characteristic drumstick form (top). Establish the position of the pivot rod and bore out the hole (bottom).

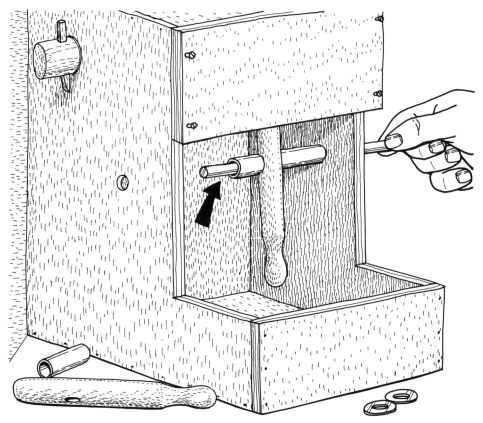

Fig. 4-8. Fitting the drumsticks. Push the pivot wire through from the side of the box and pass it through the drumsticks and spacers. Slide the washers on the rod just before you bend over the ends.

Adjusting and trimming the spacers as you go, aim for an easy but positive fit, with the two drumsticks lined up with the trip levers.

When you are pleased with the alignment of levers to drumsticks, slide the washers on the rod and bend back the ends. When you have achieved a good mechanism and the levers on the rotating shaft catch and press down on the drumsticks, attach the top front box panel.

FITTING THE DRUMSKIN

On the working drawings, notice how the leather needs to be stretched out and over the projecting open-topped part of the box. Tie the drumsticks up out of the way, then take the leather (it is best if it is slightly dampened), and pin it to the last remaining unfixed panel. This is the long edge of the panel that goes just under the drumsticks. Screw-fix the panel into position and, one side edge at a time, stretch the leather over the box and fix it with pins (FIG. 4-9). Finally, with the box right-side up on the worksurface, stretch the leather towards the front of the box, take it down over the front lip, and attach it with pins.

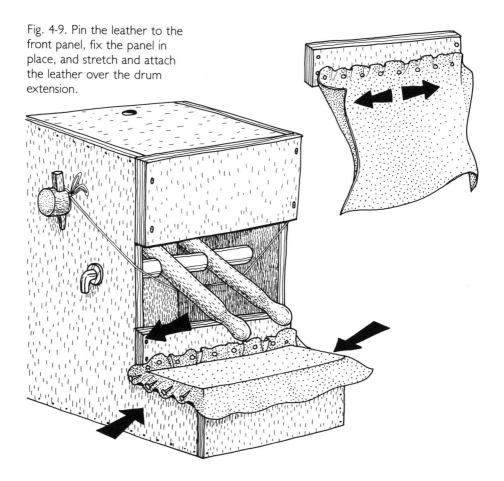

Fig. 4-9. Pin the leather to the front panel, fix the panel in place, and stretch and attach the leather over the drum extension.

CUTTING THE SAIL BLOCKS AND FITTING THE BLADES

Take the 16-inch piece of 2-×-1-inch hardwood, cut it in half, and—one piece at a time—mark each half off at 2 inches, 1 inch, 2 inches, 1 inch, and 2 inches. Use the straight saw and the chisel to lower the central 2-inch area by $1/2$ inch. Work both pieces of wood so that they lap together to make a cross (FIG. 4-10). Now, bearing in mind that the sail needs to turn in a counter-clockwise direction, mark off the 2-inch end piece of each arm, and use the saw and the chisel to bevel each face.

When you have cut and worked both lengths of wood that go to make up the sail block cross, glue and pin them together, and use the 1-inch bit to bore out the drive shaft hole. Screw three of the sail blades in place on the bevels, slide the washer on the drive shaft, screw the sail hub to the shaft (FIG. 4-11), and then fit the fourth blade. Finally, rub the whole sail down to a smooth finish.

PAINTING AND FITTING

Rub the whole project down with the graded sandpapers—smooth the cut edges and round off the corners and angles of the box. This done, wipe away all the dust

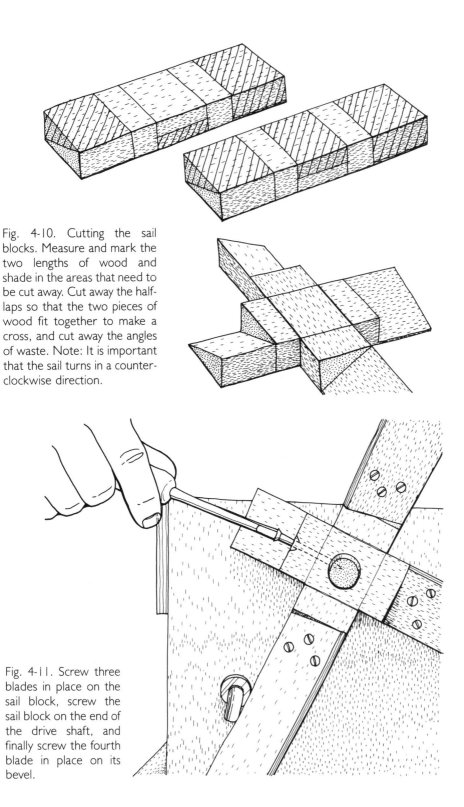

Fig. 4-10. Cutting the sail blocks. Measure and mark the two lengths of wood and shade in the areas that need to be cut away. Cut away the half-laps so that the two pieces of wood fit together to make a cross, and cut away the angles of waste. Note: It is important that the sail turns in a counter-clockwise direction.

Fig. 4-11. Screw three blades in place on the sail block, screw the sail block on the end of the drive shaft, and finally screw the fourth blade in place on its bevel.

and debris, and retreat to the dust-free area that you have set aside for painting.

Being careful not to get paint on the leather, pick out all the details and patterns that go to make up the design. When the acrylic paint is dry, lay on two coats of clear varnish.

While the varnish is drying, select a stout post and sink a $1/2$-inch-diameter hole down into the top of it to a depth of $7-8$ inches. Next, take the 24-inch length of $1/2$-inch rod and bang it down into the hole $9-10$ inches (FIG. 4-12). Drill out a few hardwood off-cuts and slide them down over the shaft.

Finally, grease the shaft and the hardwood distance pieces. Slide and locate the wind machine on the shaft—then stand well back, and enjoy your work of art!

HINTS AND MODIFICATIONS

Only use best-quality, exterior grade multicore plywood. If you use particle board or softcore board, the project will warp and break up when it gets wet.

If you want to modify the design to have four or more drumsticks, make a full-size prototype/working model with cardboard and experiment with the trip levers and see if you can achieve an authentic drum roll.

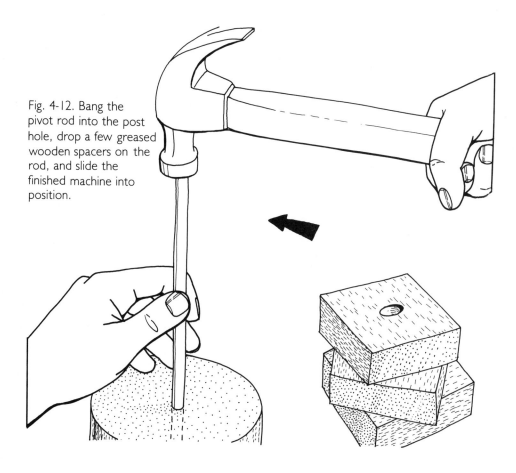

Fig. 4-12. Bang the pivot rod into the post hole, drop a few greased wooden spacers on the rod, and slide the finished machine into position.

If you don't like the idea of a leather drumskin, you could use a sheet of thin tinplate—a biscuit tin lid or even stiff plastic.

When you are varnishing the project, be sure to generously cover all the cut edges. Apply varnish in a warm, dry atmosphere.

Bear in mind that the sail blades will be turning at a powerful speed and make sure that they are well above head height or that the machine is fenced off.

Tubular bells windmill

The smooth, soft sound of tiny ting-a-ling bells and the soft swish of the turning sails makes this wind machine a piece of musical sculpture (FIG. 5-1). The movement is beautifully direct and simple: Inside the windmill box, there are two leather and brass bell clappers and a length of brass tube. As the shaft turns, the bell clappers flip around and come into contact with the tube.

When and where wind machines of this type and character first came into being is uncertain. The windmill shape appears Dutch, and the decoration seems to draw its inspiration from Pennsylvanian Dutch hex motifs. Using the wind to make music is probably oriental in origin.

TOOLS AND MATERIALS

☐ A sheet of $1/4$-inch-thick multicore plywood for the main body of the windmill: the sides, the roof, the four sails, and the two inside-box stop rings

☐ A piece of $1/2$-inch-thick wood about 5×12 inches for the base, which can be a piece of plank or a piece of plywood

☐ A few scraps of $3/4$-inch-thick hardwood/plywood for the boss ring and the sail block

☐ A $7-8$ inch length of $3/8$-inch-diameter wooden dowel for the drive shaft

☐ A few solid brass curtain/key rings

☐ A 12-inch strip of soft $1/2$-inch-wide leather for the two bell clappers

☐ A 3-inch length of $3/4$-inch-diameter tube for the bell (brass is best)

☐ A quantity of waterproof wood glue

☐ A handful of brass pins/nails   ☐ Acrylic paint—colors to suit

☐ A can of clear varnish

☐ A large screw and three washers for the main base pivot

☐ A sheet each of graph paper and tracing paper

☐ A pencil and ruler   ☐ A try square   ☐ A straight saw

☐ A coping saw or scroll saw

☐ A hand drill with bits at $1/4$ inch, $3/8$ inch, and $1/2$ inch

☐ Screwdrivers to match the screws

☐ A pack of graded sandpaper   ☐ A knife

☐ A selection of brushes: fine, medium, and large

Fig. 5-1. This beautiful classic windmill form is decorated with traditional Pennsylvania Dutch hex motifs.

DESIGN AND TECHNIQUE

Examine the working drawings (FIGS. 5-2 and 5-3), and note how the machine is made and put together. The box is cut and pinned and the edges worked and angled to fit. The project is decorated with traditional hex designs. These are based on compass-drawn motifs, with the circles divided and subdivided, and the various areas and shapes blocked in with flat color.

CUTTING THE WOOD AND BUILDING THE BOX

When you have worked out assembly procedures, and when you have considered various options and modifications, draw the design up to full size and make a cutting plan (FIG. 5-4). Take a tracing and pencil press transfer the traced lines through to the working face of your wood. Mark in the position of the dowel and screw

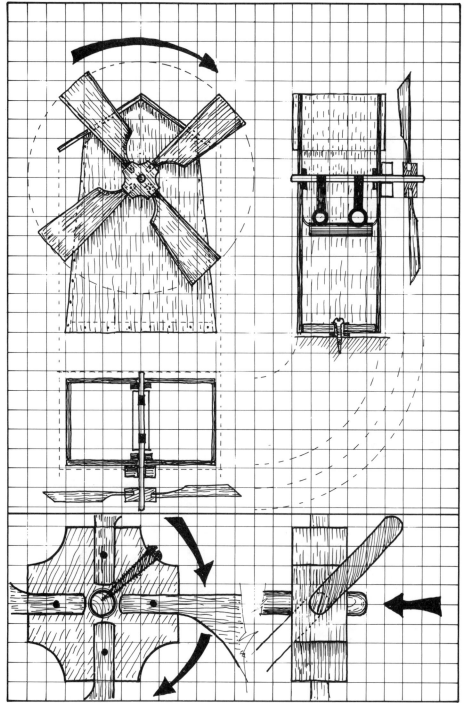

Fig. 5-2. Working drawing. At a grid scale of 1 grid square to 1 inch, the windmill measures 6 × 8 inches at the base and stands about 13 inches high. Note the simple movement and the way the wind vanes, or sails, are fixed into the sail block boss.

Fig. 5-3. Color grid. The scale is I grid square to I inch. Note that many of the designs can be drawn directly with a compass.

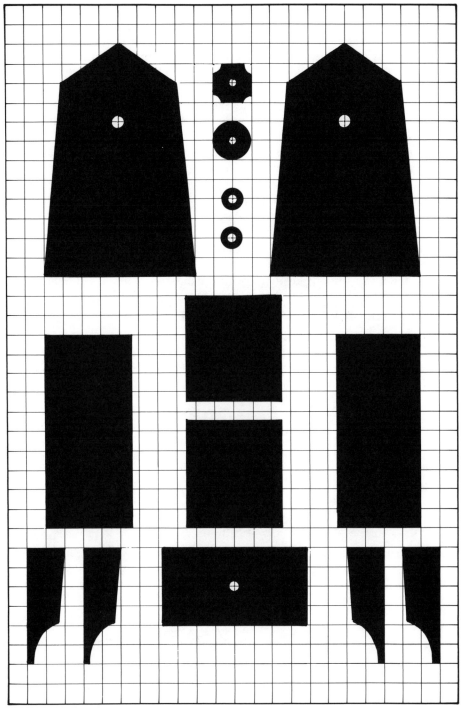

Fig. 5-4. Cutting plan. The scale is 1 grid square to 1 inch.

holes, and check to make sure that you haven't misread one or other of the measurements.

Now use the straight saw, and the coping saw or scroll saw to rip the wood down into easy-to-handle pieces. Use the coping saw to cut out the various profiles that go to make up the design. You will have on hand the seven pieces that go to make up the box: the two roof pieces, the four sides and the base, the two inside-box stop rings, the boss ring, the sail block, and the four sail blades. Label the cutouts with pencil so that you know exactly where they fit. Then bore out the various screw and dowel holes. Use the pack of graded sandpapers to rub the wood down to a working finish. Be careful not to overwork the edges—just remove the whiskers, strands, and splinters (FIG. 5-5).

When the wood has been roughed out, take the five pieces that go to make up the main box shell: the base and the four sides. With the back of the box set flat down on the workbench, start to glue and pin the box together. Fit and pin the bottom between the sides and the front onto the sides (FIG. 5-6). Refer to the working drawings and see how you need to slope and angle some of the butted joints to fit. Finally, when the glue is set, take the graded sandpapers and rub the jointed corners down to a smooth, ready-to-paint finish.

FITTING THE DRIVE SHAFT AND THE BELL

Set the partially built windmill box with the base side down on the workbench, and check that the two $1/2$-inch-diameter drive shaft holes are well aligned. Slide the $3/8$-inch diameter dowel through the box and make sure that it is a loose, easy-

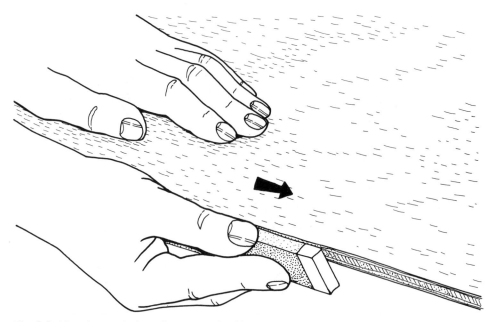

Fig. 5-5. Use the graded sandpapers and a block to rub the cut ply edges down to a swift working finish. Be careful not to overwork the edges and so blur the angles.

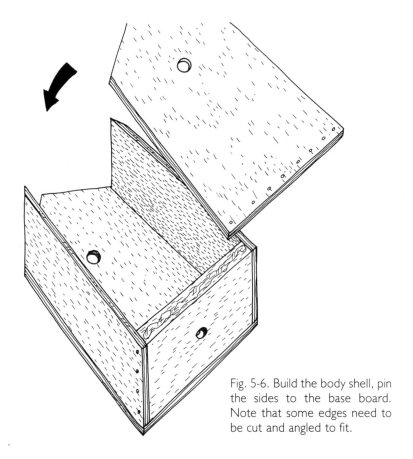

Fig. 5-6. Build the body shell, pin the sides to the base board. Note that some edges need to be cut and angled to fit.

to-turn fit. Take the dowel out of the box and at the same time, slide the dowel through the box and through the two stop rings (FIG. 5-7). Set the rings so that only about ¹/₂ inch of dowel sticks out at the back of the box. Attach them with glue and pins.

With the drive shaft a loose, easy fit, thread a short length of cord through the tube bell. Hang it from the sides of the box so that it is about 2¹/₂ – 3 inches under the shaft. Now take the two heavy brass curtain rings, the soft strip leather and the glue, and make the two bell clappers. Set the rings so that they are just touching the tube, and glue the leather to the shaft and to the rings. It's a good idea—just in case the glue works loose—to also fit the leather to the shaft with a few pins. If all is well, as the shaft turns the rings should flip over and strike the tube (FIG. 5-8). Finally, slide the boss ring on the shaft at the front of the box, and fix it with a dab of glue.

MAKING AND FITTING THE SAILS

Locate a 2-×-2 inch square, ³/₄-inch-thick piece of hardwood for the sailblock. Use a compass, pencil, and ruler to mark out all the sizes, holes, and curves that make up the design (FIG. 5-9). The shaft hole needs to be ³/₈ inch in diameter and

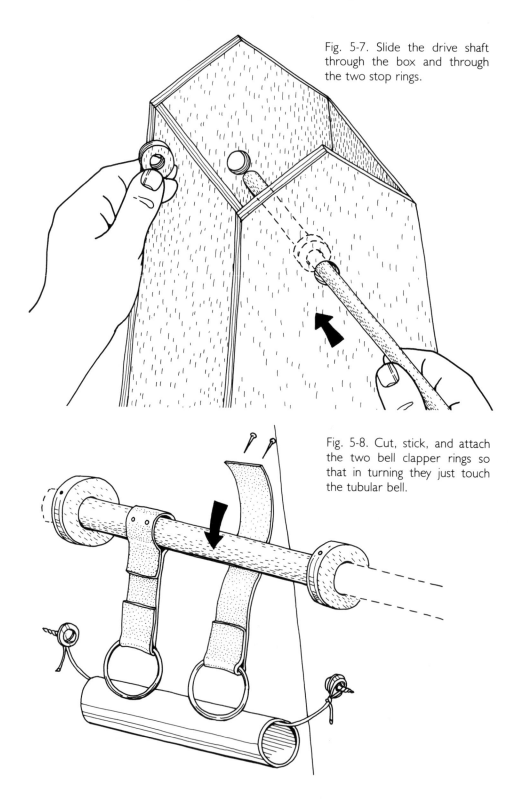

Fig. 5-7. Slide the drive shaft through the box and through the two stop rings.

Fig. 5-8. Cut, stick, and attach the two bell clapper rings so that in turning they just touch the tubular bell.

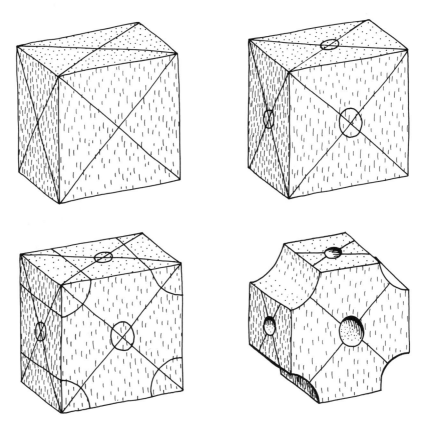

Fig. 5-9. Fitting the sails. Draw crossed diagonals to find the center point (top left). Mark out the hole sizes—the drive shaft needs to be $^3/_8$ inch in diameter and the sails $^1/_4$ inch (top right). Use a compass to draw out the corner scoops (bottom left). Clear the waste with the drills and the coping saw (bottom right).

the sail holes $^1/_4$ inch in diameter. Mark out the corner scoops with the compass set at a radius of $^1/_2$ inch, and with the compass point centered on the corner of the block. Clear the waste with the drill and the coping saw. Rub the resultant cross-shaped form to a smooth finish with the graded sandpapers.

With coping saw, knife, and sandpaper, work the four marked-out sail blades to a smooth, round-edged finish. Round off the long shaft or shank at the tapered end of each sail (FIG. 5-10). With all four sail blades a tight push fit in the sail block, set them so that they are all looking in the same direction. Angle up the short trailing edge of each blade, and attach with glue and pins.

PAINTING, FITTING, AND FINISHING

When you have the main units that go to make up the project—the box with the fitted shaft, the sails and block, and the roof boards—wipe them with a slightly damp cloth and set them out for painting. Lay on a primer, an undercoat, and a topcoat. Don't forget to let the paint dry out between coats. When the topcoat is

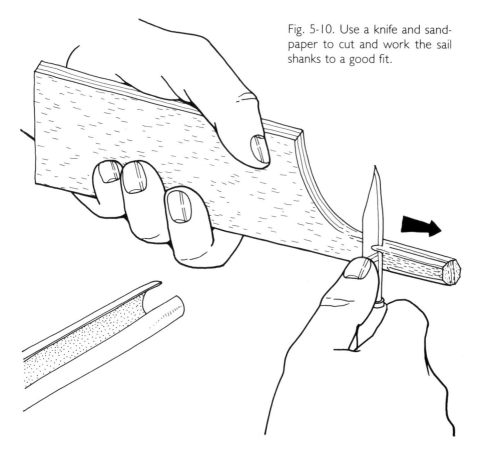

Fig. 5-10. Use a knife and sandpaper to cut and work the sail shanks to a good fit.

dry, use a compass to set out the various hex motifs (FIG. 5-11). Use a fine point brush and the colors of your choice to block in all the patterns that go to make up the design. When the paint is completely dry, lay on a few coats of varnish.

While the varnish is drying, look outside for a suitable fixing point. The top of a broad post or the top of a flat roof is best. Using a long brass/bronze screw, two washers, and a long screwdriver, screw the mill down through the base hole and into position. Make sure that both washers are greased and place them each side of the base.

Finally, when the mill is securely fit, pin down the two roof boards (FIG. 5-12). Slide the sail block onto the end of the shaft and drive home the brass fixing screw. The roof will be easier to fit if you have a pencil guide line under the roof overhang.

HINTS AND MODIFICATIONS

At about 13 – 14 inches high, this is one of the smallest machines in the book. You could double it up in size and fit a more complicated chime of bells.

You could fit pulley wheels to the main shaft and use them to drive a secondary movement. Use a belt-operated figure or perhaps a larger bell.

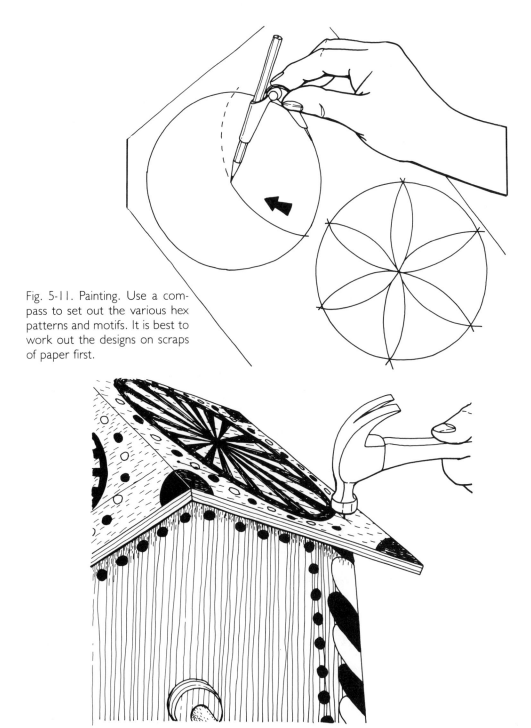

Fig. 5-11. Painting. Use a compass to set out the various hex patterns and motifs. It is best to work out the designs on scraps of paper first.

Fig. 5-12. When everything has been fitted and decorated, pin the two roof boards in place and touch up any damaged areas with paint.

After assembly, you might paint nail and screw heads and areas that have been scuffed. Although acrylic paint is easy and swift to use, it does have to be well protected with clear varnish. Make sure that the wood and the paint are completely dry before you lay on the varnish.

Clown on an English penny-farthing bike windmill

Known in England as a "penny-farthing" and in America as an "ordinary," this huge bike is one of the biggest, best, most dangerous, and most exciting bicycles of all time. Can you imagine sitting about 15 feet off the ground and traveling along on a machine that has solid tires, hit-and-miss brakes, and a fixed-wheel drive? No wonder early cyclists were thought to be dare-devil exhibitionists (FIG. 6-1).

The bicycle was called a penny-farthing in England because the two wheels— one large and the other small—were compared to a large penny coin and a small farthing. The penny-farthing windmill draws its inspiration from Victorian sand toys, where figures and objects are set into motion, not by wind, but by a trickle of sand falling onto a paddle or bucket wheel. With this particular windmill, the illusion is perfect: When the wheel is set in motion, it really does look as if the clown is pedaling away for all he is worth. It is a wonderful machine!

TOOLS AND MATERIALS
- [ ] A piece of 1/2-inch-thick multicore plywood about 24×36 inches, for all the wooden cutouts that go to make up the project
- [ ] A piece of 1-×-1-inch square pine about 8 inches long for the base
- [ ] A thin wire coathanger for the various pivots and pedals
- [ ] A sheet of thin tinplate, copper, or aluminum about 5 inches square, for the wheel
- [ ] A handful of small brass washers to fit the pivot wire
- [ ] A small amount of waterproof glue
- [ ] A small amount of two-tube resin glue for the wood-to-metal joints
- [ ] Acrylic paint, colors to suit   [ ] A can of clear yacht varnish
- [ ] A sheet each of graph paper and tracing paper
- [ ] A pencil and ruler   [ ] A compass   [ ] A coping saw or scroll saw
- [ ] A pack of graded sandpapers
- [ ] A small pair of tin snips or shears, or a pair of old scissors
- [ ] An electric soldering iron

(Continued)

☐ A hand drill with a good selection of drill bits
☐ A pair of long-nose pliers
☐ A selection of broad and fine-point paint brushes

Fig. 6-1. A delightful windmill automation that draws its inspiration from traditional Victorian sand toys.

DESIGN AND TECHNIQUE

Examine the working drawings (FIGS. 6-2, 6-3, and 6-4). Note the cranked wire for the foot pedals and the loop-end fixing for the various easy-fit pivots. The disc of tin has been divided into eight equal segments, and cut and bent to make the sail wheel. The wheel has been sandwiched between two plywood hub rings and

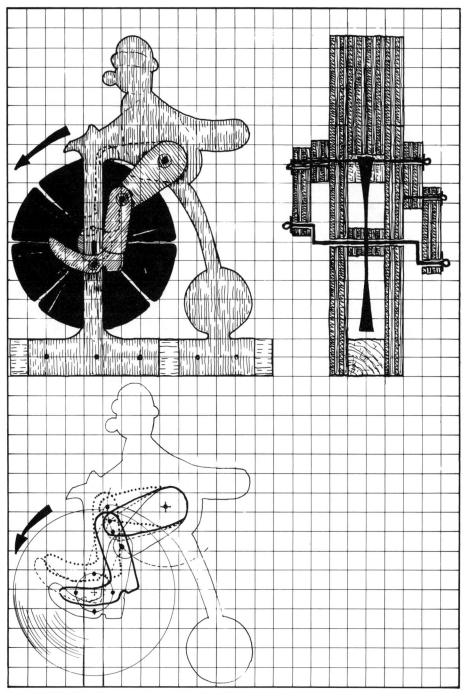

Fig. 6-2. Working drawing. At a grid scale of 2 grid squares to 1 inch, the workpiece stands about 9 inches high and 7 inches wide. Note the three-pivot leg movement, the tin disc that needs to be cut and bent, and the way the whole form can easily be fretted without removing the coping saw blade from its frame.

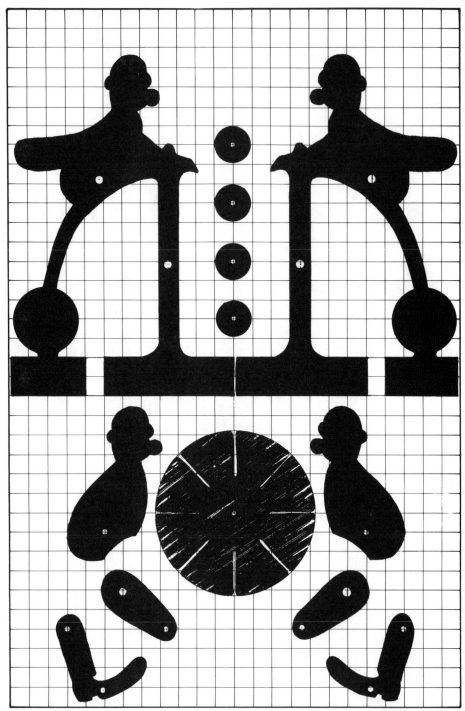

Fig. 6-3. Cutting grid. The scale is 2 grid squares to 1 inch. Note: The washers are quite difficult to cut—make four and then use the best two. The sail disc needs to be made from thin metal sheet.

Fig. 6-4. Painting grid. The scale is 4 grid squares to 1 inch.

fixed with glue and pins. Note how, as the wind drives the wheel, so the wheel turns and crank-operates the clown's two loosely pivoted legs.

SETTING UP AND CUTTING

When you have a good understanding of how the project works and is assembled, as well as how it might be improved and modified, then draw the design up to full size. Pencil press transfer the lines of the design through to the working face of the $1/4$-inch-thick plywood and the tinplate. Label the shapes so that you know exactly where they fit in the scheme of things. Check the position of all the pivot points, and note how some pivots need to be a loose fit. Then take the hand drill and the bits best suited to the diameter of your coathanger wire, and bore out all the holes (FIG. 6-5).

Cut the wood swiftly down into manageable pieces and use the coping saw or scroll saw to cut out the shapes that go to make up the design. Make sure, when you are using the saw, that the wood is well secured and the blade is set to pass

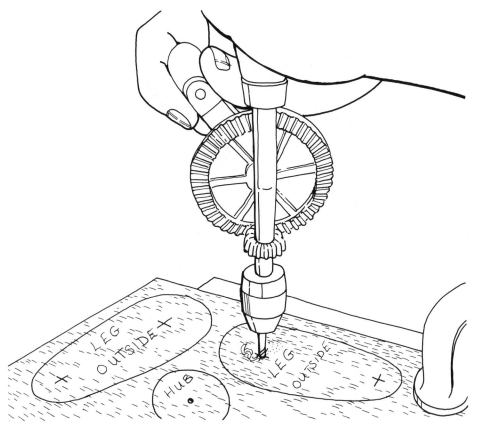

Fig. 6-5. Bore out the various holes with a hand drill. Have the wood backed with a scrap waster and secured with a clamp, so the wood won't split and splinter as the drill breaks through.

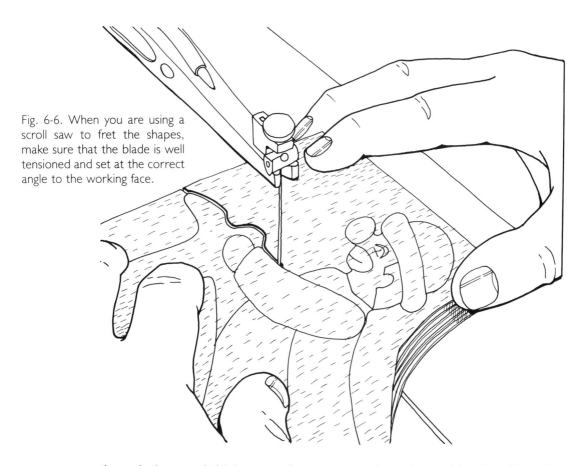

Fig. 6-6. When you are using a scroll saw to fret the shapes, make sure that the blade is well tensioned and set at the correct angle to the working face.

through the wood thickness at the correct angle to the working face. Note that some edges are cut at an angle of less than 90° (FIG. 6-6). Aim for cutouts that are smoothly worked and have crisp edges.

Finally, use the graded sandpapers to rub the wood down to a smooth, splinter-free, ready-to-paint finish.

BUILDING AND PAINTING

Take the four cutouts that go to make up the integral body and frame—the two large body/bike sides and the two body/head spacers—and set them out on the worksurface. Sandwich the four pieces of wood up in the correct order: body/bike, body/head, body/head, body/bike. When you have achieved a nicely layered stack, smear the mating faces with glue and clamp them together (FIG. 6-7).

Set the tinplate out on the worksurface, and with the compass set to a radius of $2^{1}/8$ inches, scribe out a crisp $4^{1}/4$-inch diameter circle. This done, reset the compass to a radius of about $^{3}/4$ inch and draw in a $1^{1}/2$-inch-diameter inner circle. Use a pencil, ruler, and compass to mark in the eight side-to-center sail divisions. Reduce the two hub rings to a thickness of $^{3}/8$ inch. Glue two 1-inch-diameter hub rings, set them each side of the tin (meaning each side of the center

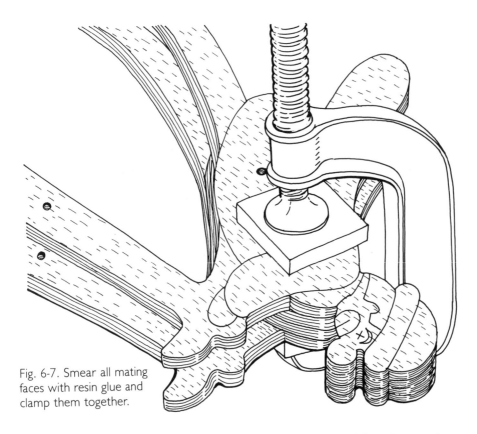

Fig. 6-7. Smear all mating faces with resin glue and clamp them together.

point), and fix them with a couple of small pins or nails. The pins need to go a good way through the ply-tin-ply sandwich.

When the resin glue is set, use the tin snips to cut in from side to center along each of the eight radial lines. Stop when the cut reaches the inner ring (FIG. 6-8). Now hold the wheel so that you can see it face on, and—being very careful not to cut yourself on the sharp edges—work around from segment to segment, angling the tin so that the left hand edge of each sail looks away from you.

Finally, when you have built the body frame, the wheel, and the leg sections, set them up in a dust-free area. Lay on a primer, an undercoat, top coat, and all the small decorative details that go to make up the design. Don't forget to let the paint dry out between coats.

MAKING THE PEDAL CRANK

When the paint is completely dry, set out the wheel, 3 – 4 inches of coathanger wire, the main body frame, and the pliers. Dab a little resin glue inside the hub hole at each side of the wheel (FIG. 6-9), and with the wheel set between the forks, use the pliers to push the length of wire through the fork bearing holes and through the hub. Aim for a wire that is a tight fit through the wheel and a loose fit through the forks. See to it that there is a good length of wire at each side of the wheel.

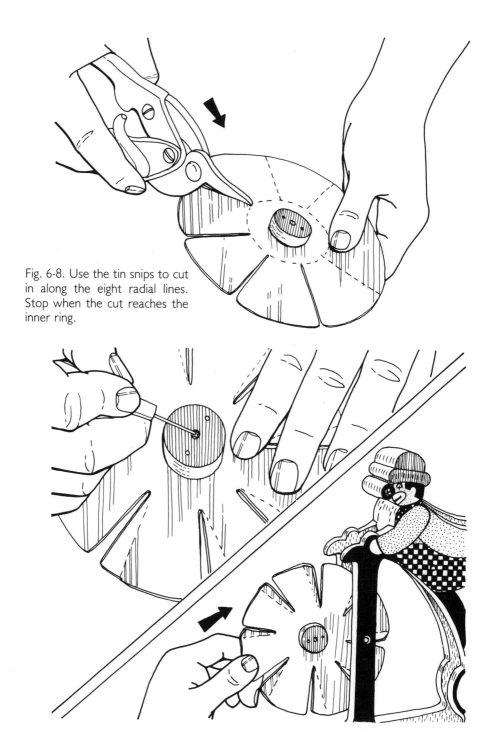

Fig. 6-8. Use the tin snips to cut in along the eight radial lines. Stop when the cut reaches the inner ring.

Fig. 6-9. Making the pedal crank. Dab a little resin glue into the hub hole at each side of the wheel (top left). Carefully position the wheel between the two forks (bottom right).

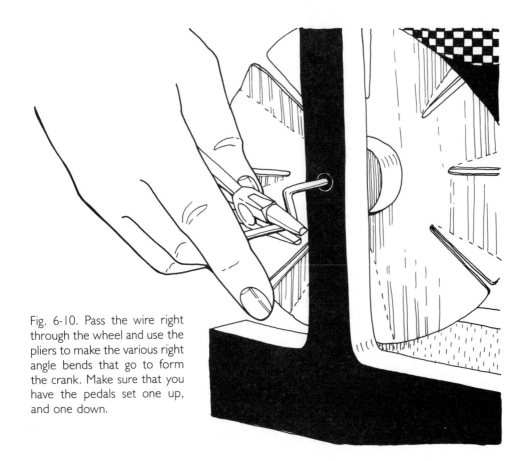

Fig. 6-10. Pass the wire right through the wheel and use the pliers to make the various right angle bends that go to form the crank. Make sure that you have the pedals set one up, and one down.

When the resin glue is set, examine the working drawing details to see how the crank needs to be worked. Note the spacing between the bicycle forks and the clown's feet, and use the pliers to make the various 90° bends in the wire that go to make up the design (FIG. 6-10). As you are bending the wire, make sure you don't twist the forks and split the wood. If necessary, have a helper support the main body of the project while you bend the wire.

FITTING THE PIVOTS AND FINISHING

When you have shaped the crank, look at the working drawing details again to see how the hip pivot goes right through all seven layers of plywood. The wire is a tight fit through the body and a loose fit through the thighs, while the knee pivot wire needs to be a flush fit at the back of the leg. The legs pieces are stepped out from thigh to foot, so the feet are on the outside.

Starting with the knee joint, cut two short wire pivots and, one piece at a time, solder a blob on one end and push the wire through from the back of the leg. Push the soldered blob or head down into the wood until it is flush. Fit the lower leg and the washer and secure by bending the wire to form a loop (FIG. 6-11). Make sure that the legs are on the right way, fit the pedal cranks through the foot

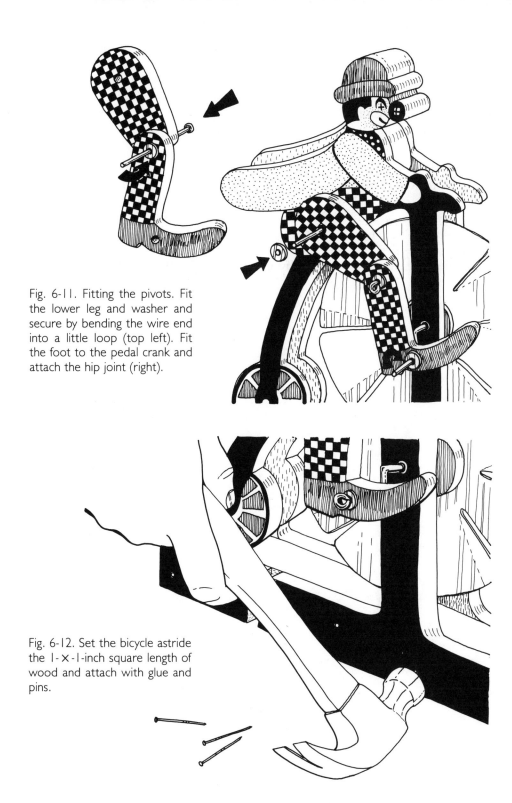

Fig. 6-11. Fitting the pivots. Fit the lower leg and washer and secure by bending the wire end into a little loop (top left). Fit the foot to the pedal crank and attach the hip joint (right).

Fig. 6-12. Set the bicycle astride the 1-×-1-inch square length of wood and attach with glue and pins.

holes, and pass the hip wire from leg to leg through the body. Secure the various pivot ends by bending and looping the wire. Remember to fit the washers.

When all the pivot wires have been fitted and the working action of the legs tested and adjusted, set the bicycle astride the length of 1-x-1-inch-square wood. Attach with glue and pins (FIG. 6-12). Finally, bolt the project in an exposed position and let the wind catch and turn the wheel as it may.

HINTS AND MODIFICATIONS

Using $^1/_2$-inch-thick plywood, our project measures about 9 inches high and 6 inches long—from the clown's coat tails to the front of the wheel—and about $4^1/_2$ inches wide. You could modify the design by using thicker ply, and by doubling up the scale so that it is 18 inches high.

The tin is sharp edged; you could roll the outer edge.

You could simplify assembly by using nuts and bolts for the pivots rather than wire.

7

Dutch windmill weathervane

In days gone by, almost every house and cottage would have boasted a weather-vane. If old prints are to be believed, the skyline must have been awash with angels, trains, horses, Indians, roosters, peacocks, and other dramatically silhouetted shapes. Of course, weathervanes were not only popular because they were decorative; they were also functional. A well-placed weathervane provided a reliable weather report. Considering how many people were either sailors or farmers, existence was often determined by the weather.

This is probably the easiest project in the book. If you are a beginner, this one is for you (FIG. 7-1).

TOOLS AND MATERIALS

☐ A large sheet each of graph paper and tracing paper   ☐ A roll of masking tape
☐ A sheet of $1/2$-inch-thick multicore plywood, 36×24 inches
☐ A 72-inch length of 3-×-1-inch hardwood
☐ Four 12-inch lengths of $1/4$-inch-diameter galvanized metal rod
☐ A 12-inch length of threaded $3/8$-inch-diameter stainless steel rod, with four nuts, two plain washers, one large brass washer, and two lock washers to fit
☐ Resin glue   ☐ A dozen or so 2-inch-long brass screws   ☐ A can of heavy-duty wood primer
☐ A can of black enamel paint   ☐ A can of varnish   ☐ A pencil and ruler
☐ A straight saw   ☐ A coping saw or scroll saw
☐ A hand drill with bits at $1/8$-inch, $1/4$-inch, $1/2$-inch and $11/2$-inches. The $1/2$-inch bit must have a long reach, and the $11/2$-inch bit needs to be an auger or a sawtooth
☐ A plane   ☐ A pack of graded sandpapers   ☐ A hack saw
☐ A screwdriver   ☐ A few spanners to fit the nuts
☐ A clamp   ☐ A few medium-size paint brushes
☐ Odds and ends such as turps, tubs, newspaper, pliers, and old cloths

DESIGN AND TECHNIQUE

Examine the working drawings (FIGS. 7-2 and 7-3). The weathervane design is simple and traditional. Note the Dutch imagery, the bold silhouette form, and the easy-to-make, nuts-and-bolts pivot.

Fig. 7-1. A beautiful functional weathervane with Dutch imagery. Note the easy-to-make structure and the visual balance of the silhouette.

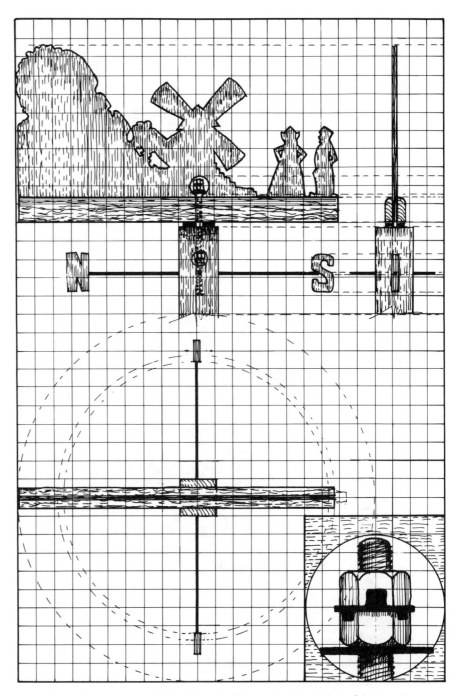

Fig. 7-2. Working drawing. At a grid scale of about 1 grid square to 2 inches, the vane measures 36 inches long. Note the way the plywood cutout is fixed and supported, and how the weathervane is pivoted to the post. The scale of the bottom right hand detail is 4 grid squares to 1 inch.

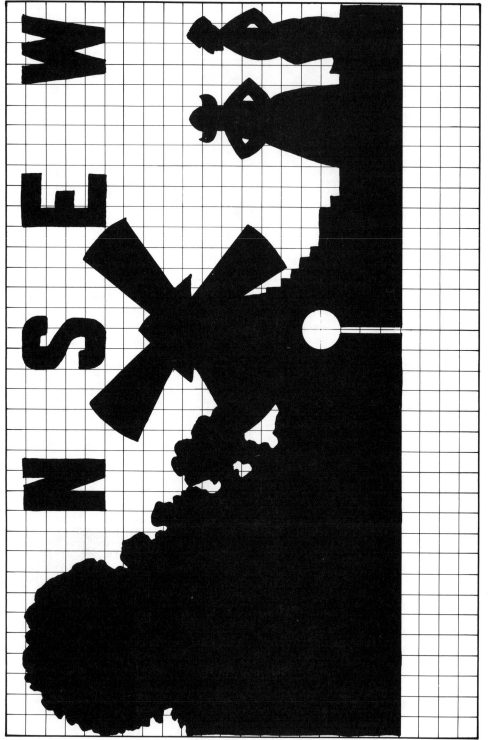

Fig. 7-3. Cutting grid. The grid scale is 1 grid square to 1 inch.

If, after studying the design, you like the overall idea of the project but want to make changes, simply try to achieve the same sort of balance and proportions. For example, if you want a figure or animal in the pioneer tradition rather than the Dutch scene, bear in mind that the pivot point must be off center and set slightly nearer the end that you want to veer into the wind.

With this project, the mounting post pivotal fixing needs to be extra secure. This is not to say that, with the other projects, the pivot or swing points can be sloppy or unsafe. However, because the weathervane really must be set high up to catch the wind, it is important that the fixings be strong and stable. Note the need for lock washers.

CUTTING OUT

When you have a good idea of how your weathervane will be, draw the design up to full size (FIG. 7-3) and take a tracing. Bear in mind that the timber needs to be of top quality—free from stains, splits, dead knots, and cracks. Secure the tracing

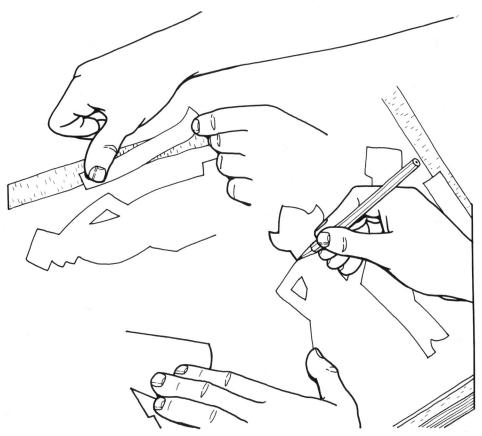

Fig. 7-4. When you have traced off the design, pencil over the back of the design and tape the tracing directly to the working surface of the plywood (top). With the tracing well secured, pencil press transfer the traced lines through to the wood (bottom).

with tabs of sticky tape (FIG. 7-4, top) and pencil press transfer the traced lines through to the face of the wood (FIG. 7-4, bottom).

Be careful not to split or splinter the plywood, and take the straight saw and rip the wood down into its component parts. Then use the coping saw or a scroll saw to cut out all the fine forms, the main silhouette, and the letters. Cut on the waste side of the drawn line, making sure that the blade passes through the wood at right angles to the working face (FIG. 7-5). For pierced areas, you will need to drill starter holes and remove the blade from the saw frame.

When you have cut out the seven parts that go to make up the project—the silhouette cutout, the four letters, and the two long base or strengthener strips—use the graded sandpapers to rub all the cut edges down to a smooth, slightly rounded finish. Pay particular attention to the outside top edges of the two long base strips; they need to be well rounded in section so as to throw off water. It is best to draw guide lines and use the plane to clear away the main strip of waste (FIG. 7-6), then to use sandpaper to achieve the smooth, rounded finish.

MAKING THE VANE AND PAINTING

First check that the threaded stainless steel rod is a loose fit in the pivot slot. Then take the main silhouette and the two 36-inch-long, 1-x-3-inch base strips, and set

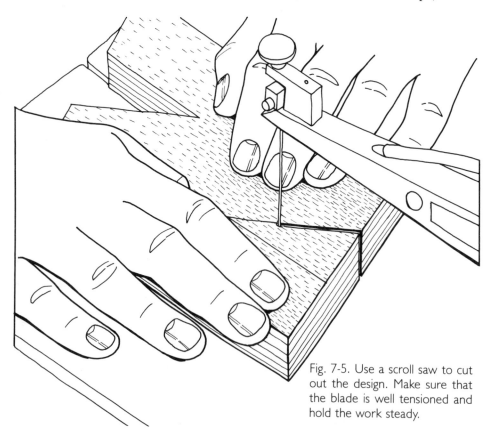

Fig. 7-5. Use a scroll saw to cut out the design. Make sure that the blade is well tensioned and hold the work steady.

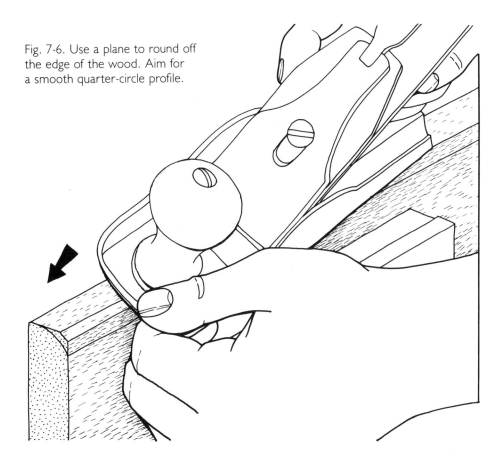

Fig. 7-6. Use a plane to round off the edge of the wood. Aim for a smooth quarter-circle profile.

them out in the correct order. Double check the working drawing details to make sure all is correct, then smear all mating faces with a generous amount of resin glue and clamp up. With the wood well secured, mark off both sides of the base at 6-inch intervals, drill pilot holes, and run screws through the three-layer sandwich (FIG. 7-7). From side to side, it is best to have the screws staggered so that they are set about 3 inches apart.

Arrange the four letter cutouts in a circle. Set them in a North, East, South, West sequence so that they are standing upright, and so that one of the long side edges of each letter looks toward center (FIG. 7-8, top). When you have established the edges facing center, mark a point halfway up their height. Then use the $^1/_4$-inch bit and drill a hole through the wood and into the body of the letter. One piece at a time, cut the $^1/_4$-inch diameter rods to size, daub their ends with resin glue, and push them into the letters (FIG. 7-8, bottom). When the glue is dry, remove the clamps and chip any dry runs or blobs of hard glue off both the vane and the letters. Fill any uneven or chipped edges with body filler and sand down to a smooth finish.

Remove the workpiece to the dust-free area or corner that you have set aside for painting. Remember that the paint must dry out between coats, and that you

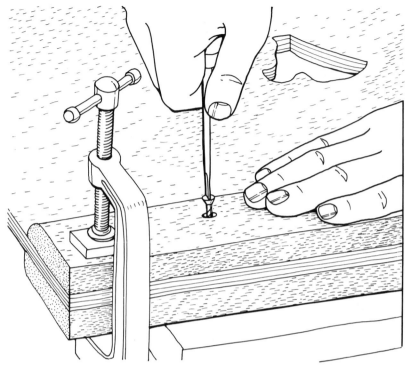

Fig. 7-7. Smear glue on all the mating faces and clamp. Then run brass screws through the layers at 3-inch intervals.

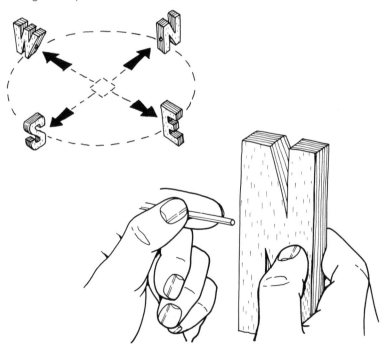

Fig. 7-8. Set the letter forms out in a points-of-the-compass circle, and mark in the position of the 1/4-inch-diameter rod support holes (top). Bore out the holes and attach the support rods with resin glue (bottom).

must work the paint well into the end grain and the cut edges. Lay on a generous coat of wood primer, at least two undercoats, and the black gloss enamel top coats. Finally, lay on a coat of varnish to make the project truly waterproof.

ASSEMBLY

The vane is best mounted on a stout post, pole, or roof finial—meaning a post that is about 4 × 4 inches square. When you have selected such a post, establish its top center point by drawing crossed diagonals, then make a mark on the side of the post about 4 inches from the top. Use the hand drill and the long-shanked, $^1/_2$-inch-diameter bit, and center the bit on the top of the post. Run a hole straight down into the body of the wood, to a depth of about 8 inches. Next, take the drill and the $1^1/_2$-inch diameter auger bit; or machine tooth saw bit. With the point set on the side mark, run a hole straight through the post thickness. Refer to the drawing details and see how the two holes need to cross at right angles to each other (FIG. 7-9).

When you have bored out the holes and made sure that the nuts run smoothly on the threaded pivot bar, carefully slide the greased pivot down into the top of the post, leaving 5 – 6 inches of threaded pivot rod sticking up. The

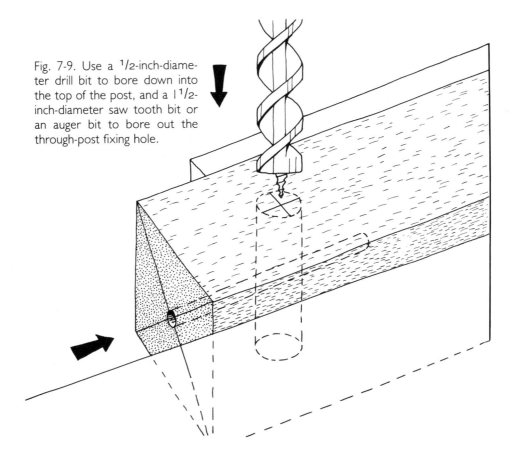

Fig. 7-9. Use a $^1/_2$-inch-diameter drill bit to bore down into the top of the post, and a $1^1/_2$-inch-diameter saw tooth bit or an auger bit to bore out the through-post fixing hole.

next part is tricky; you might need a helper. Slide the washer, nuts, and the lock washer along the 1½-inch bore hole (FIG. 7-10, left) and use your fingertips to screw fit them onto the rod. With the lock washer sandwiched between the two nuts, use two spanners to screw the nuts tightly against the lock washer (FIG. 7-10, right). With the two bottom nuts locked into position, slide the large brass washer and then the weathervane into position onto the pivot. Secure the whole works with the other nut, lock washer, and nut sandwich. Use a screwdriver to bend the lock washer tabs over against the side of the nuts (FIG. 7-11).

From top to bottom, the order of wood, washers, and nuts is: nut, lock washer, nut, plain washer, weathervane, large washer, post top, plain washer, nut, lock washer, and nut.

When you have established the North, South, East, and West points of the compass, bore ¼-inch diameter holes into the sides of the post and glue the rod-supported letters into position. Finally, make small adjustments by bending the rods and the job is done.

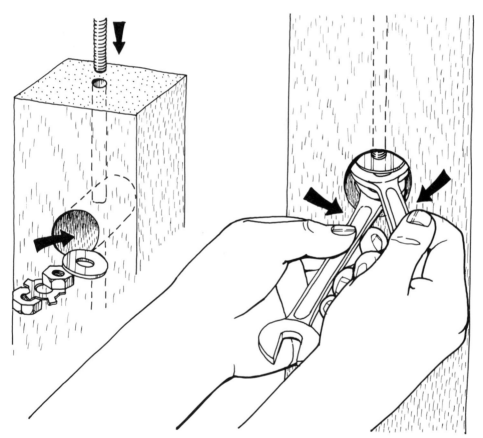

Fig. 7-10. When you have used your fingertips to thread the various nuts and washers onto the pivotal rod, use spanners to clench the nuts against the lock-washer.

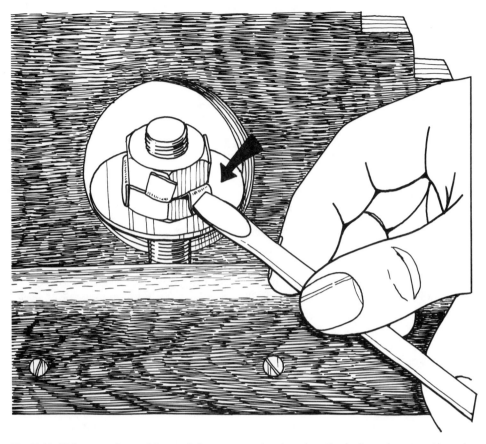

Fig. 7-11. When you have tightened the two nuts hard against the lock-washer, trap them by bending the washer tabs up and down.

HINTS AND MODIFICATIONS

If you like the idea of the weathervane, but want to make it larger or smaller, simply change the scale of the working drawing grid to fit.

If you want to make a more efficient pivot, you could drill out a $3/4$-inch diameter rod hole, line the hole with a well-greased brass or copper bush/tube, and use a slightly heavier gauge threaded rod.

When you have fitted the lock nuts you could make sure that they stay put by burring the thread with a hammer and cold chisel.

8
Man starting automobile windmill

This particular wind machine is a beauty that will amuse and interest the children, scare away seed-stealing birds, and indicate both the speed and the direction of the wind. When the blades of the windmill swing into the wind, the 1925 Chrysler sedan heads out of the weather and the man starts to swing on the starting handle. On breathless, summer days, life is easy and the man is content to quietly turn the engine over, but on windy winter days, the poor old fellow has no choice but to crank his engine for all he is worth. Of course we all know that the wind-driven crank is operating the man, rather the man operating the crank, but the movement is so lifelike, that it is difficult not to sympathize with this character (FIG. 8-1).

This particular windmill automation is a classic that has, in its many and varied forms, come to characterize most of the small, factory-made windmills that we see for sale in our catalogues and garden centers. The origin of this type of four-blade vane, crank-driven wind machine is uncertain. However, its humor and method of assembly suggests nineteenth century German-American toys.

All in all this wind machine is a real gem. It does require careful measuring and cutting, and assembly is a bit tricky, but when you can watch the man cranking the starting handle, it will all seem worthwhile!

TOOLS AND MATERIALS
- [ ] A piece of $^1/_2$-inch-thick multiply or multicore plywood, 40 inches long and 4 inches wide, for the base, strengthening quadrants, and pivot plates
- [ ] A piece of $^3/_8$-inch-thick multiply, 10 inches long and 7 inches wide, for the car
- [ ] A piece of $^3/_8$-inch-thick multiply, 10 inches long and 4 inches wide, for the man
- [ ] A piece of $^3/_8$-inch-thick multiply, 12 inches square, for the four vane blades or sails
- [ ] A piece of prepared wood, 1 × 1 inches square and 20 inches long, for the sail blocks

(Continued)

- Two 2-inch-long brass split pins with eight brass washers to fit, for the man
- A 24-inch length of $^3/_{16}$-inch-thick galvanized or brass wire with two washers to fit, for the horizontal drive
- One $^1/_2$-inch-diameter, 6-inch-long coach bolt with two washers to fit, for the main pivotal post fixing
- A small quantity of waterproof glue □ About $50 \times {}^3/_4$-inch-long brass screws
- A handful of $^3/_4$-inch-long panel pins □ Various pieces and off-cuts
- Enamel paints, colors to suit □ A can of yacht varnish
- A large sheet each of graph paper and tracing paper
- A pencil and measure □ A try square □ A compass
- A straight saw □ A coping saw
- A couple of chisels, one broad and the other narrow
- A hand drill with a good selection of drill bits
- A pair of pliers □ A hammer □ A rasp
- A pack of graded sandpapers □ A selection of paint brushes
- General workshop amenities like white spirit, old cloths, and newspapers

Fig. 8-1. This is a classic windmill design. Note the strong easy-to-make structure and the bold imagery.

DESIGN AND TECHNIQUE

Examine the working drawings and see how, apart from the sail spars, the whole project is built from plywood (FIGS. 8-2, 8-3, and 8-4).

Note the use of the two wood thicknesses: $1/2$-inch ply for the base and strengthener plates, and $3/8$-inch-ply for the man, car, and sail blades. Run your eyes over the views and sections, and see how some sizes and details are more or less fixed, while others are flexible and can be easily changed. For example, the base does need to be 18 inches long and is best made from $1/2$-inch-thick wood, but when you make the car, there's no reason why you shouldn't use a thicker or thinner material and change the design to a Ford, a Rolls, or any other car. You could change the imagery and have a man or woman cranking up a plane prop, or winding up a bucket of water from a well, or whatever—as long as the movement can be worked from a horizontal crank-end drive shaft.

Sit down with a measure, pencil, and graph paper and draw the various views and details to size. If you have any doubts as to how a certain part works or is assembled, make a mock-up. It is always a good idea to research a project by visiting folk and toy museums.

SETTING OUT THE DESIGN AND FIRST STEPS

When you have drawn the designs to full size, transfer the various profiles and images to the working face of the plywood. There should be 17 plywood elements or parts: the four sail blades, the long base, the end board or plate, two quadrants, two main pivot strengtheners, two car profiles, and the five cutouts that make up the man.

Make the best possible use of the wood, and avoid bad knots and splits. It's a good idea to label the various parts, and to code all mating edges and best faces.

Swiftly cut the plywood down into easily manageable pieces and begin cutting out the forms. The long base and the various strengthening plates are straightforward; just cut them down with a straight saw so they are crisp edged and square.

When you cut out the car or the man, take the forms one piece at a time, support them in the vise or with a clamp, and fret them out with the coping saw. It is fairly difficult to cut $3/8$-inch-thick multiply, so take it easy—work at a steady, even pace. Start at the top right, the 1 o'clock position. Be prepared to reposition the work in the vise so that the saw blade is always presented with the line of next cut. Then run the saw in a clockwise direction around the form.

Continue until you have cut out all seventeen pieces. Finally, noting which edges need to be crisp and square and which need to be rounded, use the sandpaper and block to rub the wood down to a good finish (FIG. 8-5).

BUILDING THE BASE AND FITTING THE CAR

Notice from the working drawing details that there are eight holes in the base: two mortise holes for the figure, four mortise holes for the car, a $1/2$-inch-diameter

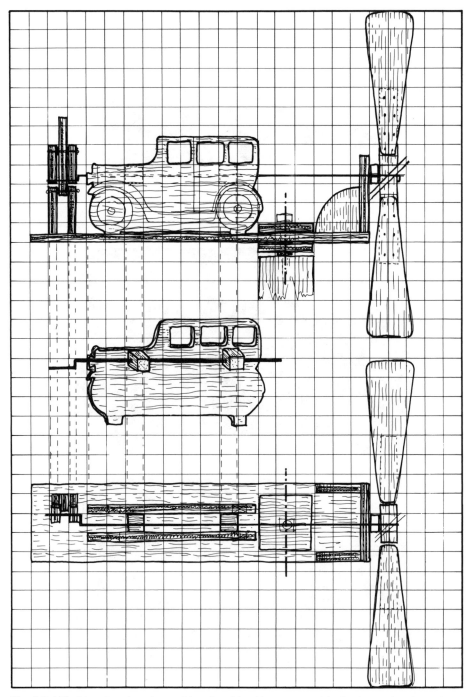

Fig. 8-2. Working drawing. At a grid scale of 1 grid square to 1 inch, the project has a base measurement of about 18 × 4 inches. Note the wire crank drive shaft and the simple nut-and-bolt post pivot.

Fig. 8-3. Cutting and painting grid. The scale is 2 grid squares to 1 inch.

Fig. 8-4. Working drawing and painting grid. The scale is 4 grid squares to 1 inch. Note the pivot fixing and the crank-operated sequence of movement.

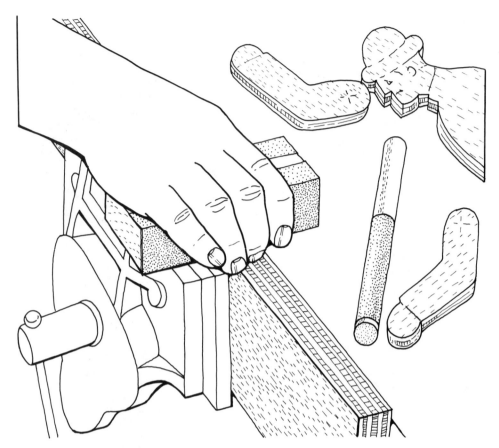

Fig. 8-5. Cut out the various forms and use a sandpaper and block to rub the edges down to a smooth finish.

hole for the coach bolt pivot, and a single loose-fit hole in the vertical end plate (FIG. 8-6). Carefully measure the tenons on the bottom of the figure and the two car profiles and chop out the six base mortises. Aim for a tight fit. Drill out the $1/2$-inch-diameter pivot hole and the drive hole.

Now take the 4-x-4-inch end plate and the two quadrants, place them square on the end of the platform, and attach with glue and pins. Next drill out the two drive blocks—which are the blocks between the cars—and use glue and pins to make the car-and-blocks sandwich.

Note that it is most important that the blocks be carefully aligned so that the drive wire can pass in a straight line from the sails through to the man (FIG. 8-7). Point the car unit in the right direction, then smear a little glue on the tenons and slot into the base.

MAKING THE SAIL BLOCKS AND FITTING THE BLADES

Take the 20-inch-long piece of 1-x-1-inch square wood and—allowing for waste—cut it down so that you have two pieces at 9 inches. Use the set square to measure

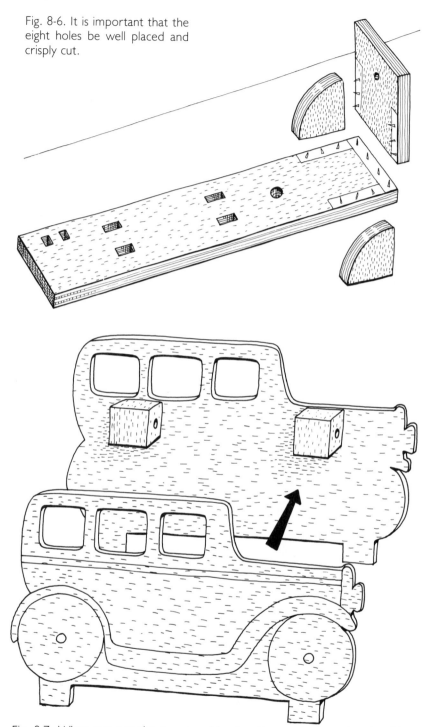

Fig. 8-6. It is important that the eight holes be well placed and crisply cut.

Fig. 8-7. When you put the two car sides together, make sure that the drive shaft blocks are well aligned.

and mark off the wood from left to right at 4 inches, $^1/_2$ inch, 1 inch, $^1/_2$ inch, and 4 inches.

Note on the working drawings and step-by-step details that the sail blocks are half-lapped and angled. Use a straight saw, mallet, and chisel to cut out the central cross half-lap and clear away the angles of waste (FIG. 8-8).

If all is correct, the half-laps should slot together to make a four-legged cross, with each leg being 4 inches long and angled or chamfered at 45°. Slot the blocks together and attach with glue and pins. Establish the center of the vane by drawing crossed diagonals. Drill out the wire drive hole and the end-of-wire location hole.

The four plywood sail blades should be 7$^1/_2$ inches long, about 3 inches wide at the broad end, tapered down to a 1 inch, and smoothly rounded at the corners. Screw them in place on the sail arms (FIG. 8-9). The four blades should be angled and fitted so that they all look in a clockwise direction.

BUILDING THE MAN

When you have built the platform base and the sails, put them to one side. Gather together all the bits and pieces that go to make up the man: the main head-torso piece, two arms, two legs, two brass split pins, and eight washers to fit the pins.

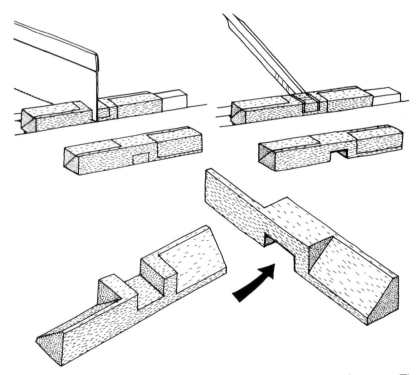

Fig. 8-8. Making the sail block. Use a saw and straight chisel to clear away the waste. The half-lap joint needs to be a tight push-fit, and when fitted, the mitred blade seatings must all be angled in the same direction.

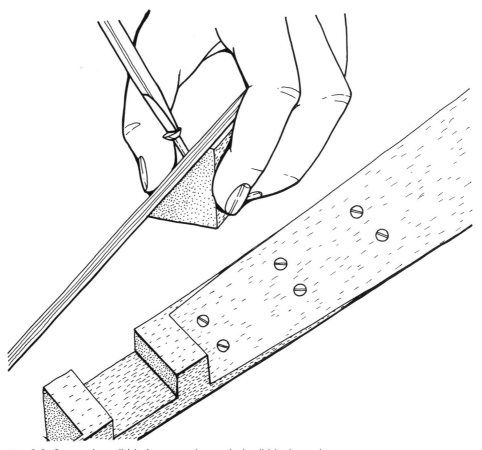

Fig. 8-9. Screw the sail blades onto the angled sail block seatings.

Start by drilling out all the pivot holes at sizes to fit the drive wire and split pins. Drill holes through the top of the legs, through the hips and shoulders, and through the top of the arms and the hands (FIG. 8-10). Rub the holes out with a scrap of sandpaper so that they are a smooth, loose fit.

Start with the arms and body, and—remembering to start and finish with a washer and to have washers between all moving parts—pass a split through the washers-and-wood sandwich and bend over the ends. To avoid wood-to-pin friction, clip the ends of the split pins back and roll them over and in towards each other, as in FIG. 8-4. Finally, trim the foot tenons to fit the base mortises.

ASSEMBLY

When you have the four main units that go to make up the project—the base, the man, the sail, and the car—then comes the slightly tricky business of putting the whole project together. It is tricky because you need to be holding the large parts steady, while at the same time trying to locate washers and holes.

Start by gluing and pinning the two 3-x-3-inch strengthener plates on each

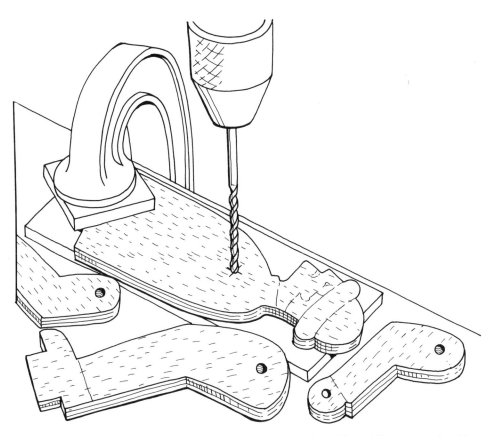

Fig. 8-10. Drill holes through the top of the arms and hands, while holding the work with a clamp.

side of the main pivot hole. Then drill a $1/2$-inch-thick, 1-x-1-inch off-cut to fit the drive wire and glue. Tack and align it in place on the front plate (FIG. 8-11). Position the base so that the front hangs over the edge of the workbench and secure it with a clamp. With pliers and washers ready, pass the drive wire through the central sail-arm hole (FIG. 8-12). Bend the end of the wire over so as to make a hook, and locate the hook in the off-center hole.

Next, slide the wire through the drive block, through the plate, and through the two car blocks. Pull on the wire so that the sail is tightly against front plate, and about halfway between the front of the car and the man's left arm. Bend the wire at right angles. Now, no more than $1/2$ inch from the first bend, make another right-angled bend so that the tail end of the wire is parallel to the main drive. If you turn the sail, the little $1/2$-inch crank should sweep a 1-inch diameter circle.

Face the man in the right direction, slide the crank through his hand holes, and slide a washer on the wire. Dab a little glue on the man's foot tenons and slot him in the base. Finally, with the wire held taut, squash the end and clip off the waste (FIG. 8-13).

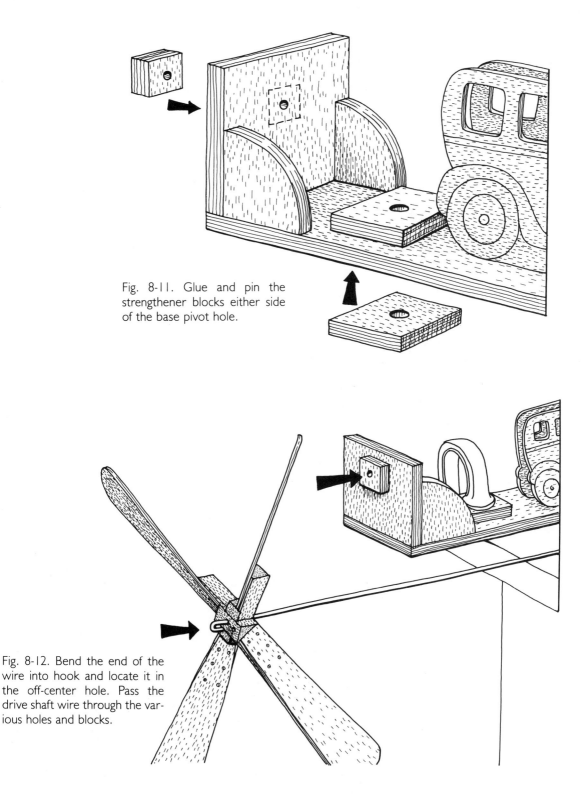

Fig. 8-11. Glue and pin the strengthener blocks either side of the base pivot hole.

Fig. 8-12. Bend the end of the wire into hook and locate it in the off-center hole. Pass the drive shaft wire through the various holes and blocks.

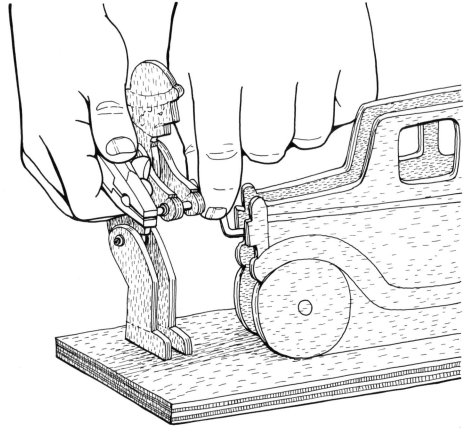

Fig. 8-13. Make the various right angled bends that go to make up the crank and pass the crank through the man's hand holes. Squeeze the end of the wire to fit and clip off the waste.

PAINTING AND FINISHING

When the glue is dry, give the sail a couple of turns. The crank should rotate on its axis and set the little man in motion. If everything is correct, clear away all the bench clutter, sweep up all the dust, wipe the whole project over with a spirit-dampened cloth, and move to the area that you have set aside for painting.

Paying particular attention to end grain and edges, lay on a primer and two undercoats. Give the paint plenty of time to dry out between coats. Then lay on your chosen main ground colors (you might use green for the base, red for the sails, and blue for the car) in single, well-brushed, drip-free blocks. It is best to start with the figure, car, and sails, then finish up with the base.

When the main ground colors are dry, use a fine-point brush to pick out all the details that go to make up the design: the man's features; his hat, shirt, and trousers; the car wheels; the two-tone bodywork, and so on. When the enamel colors are dry, remove any hard blobs or runs. Fix any damage, and finish by laying on a couple of generous coats of varnish.

Remember to have two washers on the underside of the base, then bolt the wind machine to the top of a suitable post, dribble a little light engine oil on all the moving parts, and stand back and watch the fun.

HINTS AND MODIFICATIONS

Even though the drive rod is supported several times along its length, there is a lot of play in the sail end. You might modify the design and use a thicker drive wire, and have an extra support between the back of the car and the front plate. Strengthen the top of the post by binding it with wire or strap iron.

If you find that one end of the machine is so heavy that it dips down, screw a lead counterbalance to the other end.

When you are buying the plywood, be sure to specify types: fine layer multi-ply, exterior quality, etc.

If you don't like the idea of cutting mortise slots in the base, have blocks between the car sides and between the man's legs. Attach them by running screws up through the base board.

Hardwood is best for the sail blocks.

For best results, the wood must be regularly revarnished and the moving parts oiled. Note: when the vane is spinning around it is dangerous. The sails turn through a 16-inch-diameter circle and the whole machine pivots around at the top of the post. It might be wise to locate it a foot or so above head height, or even to fence it off.

9
Mad manikins pop-up windmill

The Mad Manikins windmill draws its inspiration from the crankshaft-operated moving toys that were made during the eighteenth century in the German district of Thuringia. These beautiful sound and movement toys, made initially for home use, were all part of a highly organized German toymaking industry that exported toys all over the world. These toys were typically made entirely from wood, bold in design, brightly painted, and clever in their working. Thuringian crankshaft toys are all the more fascinating because their mechanics are complex and usually hidden from view.

The toys were traditionally set in motion by sand trickling onto a paddle wheel, or by captive birds, mice, or beetles operating a tread mill. The crankshaft converts turning motion, by way of shafts and trip rods, into up-and-down or to-and-fro movement. As the wind pushes the sail, so the shaft turns. The four trip levers on the shaft engage—lifting and dropping the little men so that they bob up and down in strict four-time rhythm (FIG. 9-1). The mad manikins windmill is ingenious and the little men are delightfully funny. Set this wind machine up in your garden and it will give you, your family, and your friends hours of gentle pleasure.

TOOLS AND MATERIALS
- [ ] A quantity of $1/2$-inch-thick multicore plywood for the box, sails, spacers, levers, and tail. With a bit of careful cutting you should be able to work it from a 4-×-4-foot sheet
- [ ] About 6 feet of rough-sawn, 2-×-2 inch, smooth-grained pine, for the four manikins
- [ ] A 15-inch length of 1-inch-diameter broomstick dowel, for the main drive rod
- [ ] Two thin brass washers cut to fit the 1-inch-diameter broomstick dowel
- [ ] A 16-inch length of 2-×-1-inch hardwood for the sail arms
- [ ] A 24-inch length of $1/2$-inch-diameter metal rod, for the main pivot
- [ ] A 3-inch length of metal tube to slide over the $1/2$-inch rod
- [ ] A can of waterproof wood glue   [ ] About thirty $3/4$-inch-long brass screws
- [ ] A handful of $3/4$-inch-long brass panel pins   [ ] Four little brass bells

(Continued)

☐ A length of nylon string or twine for the bells   ☐ Enamel paint, colors to suit
☐ A can of yacht varnish
☐ A large sheet each of graph paper and tracing paper
☐ A pencil and measure   ☐ A try square   ☐ A compass
☐ A straight saw   ☐ A coping saw
☐ A couple of chisels, one broad and one narrow
☐ A brace with two bits, one at $^1/_2$ inch and a machine saw bit at 1 inch
☐ The use of a woodturning lathe   ☐ A plane or drawknife
☐ A selection of woodturning gouges and chisels   ☐ A hammer
☐ A rasp   ☐ A pack of graded sandpapers
☐ A selection of paint brushes   ☐ General workshop tools and materials

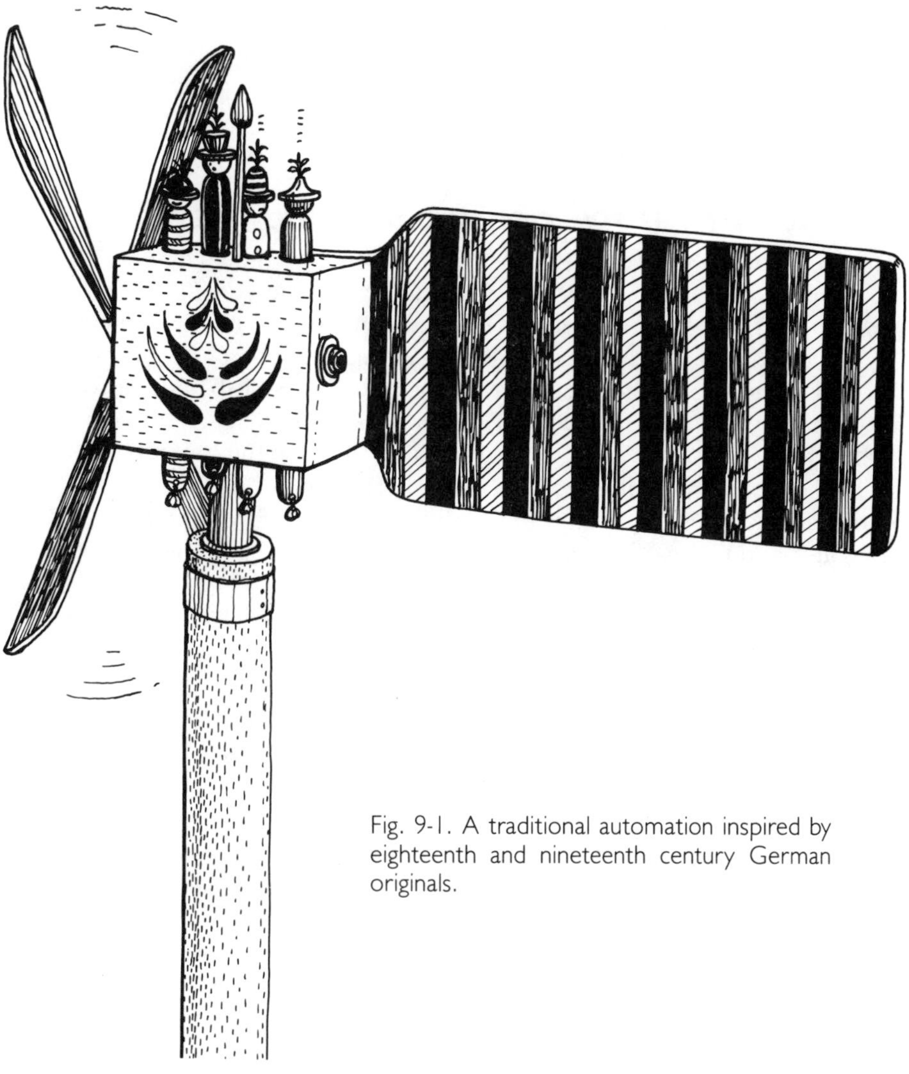

Fig. 9-1. A traditional automation inspired by eighteenth and nineteenth century German originals.

DESIGN AND TECHNIQUE

Examine the working drawings (FIGS 9-2, 9-3 and 9-4). This machine is basically assembled from 1/2-inch-thick multi-core plywood, dowels, and various turnings. Note especially how the four manikins need to be carefully turned and worked. This is not to say that the turning is complicated, only that the shoulders and stops do need to be worked to a set size and profile.

As the shaft turns, so the trip levers make contact with the trip rings (note the turned details). In practice, the shaft turns so fast that the manikins are not lifted so much as flipped. The turned rings or stops at either side of the trip ring prevent the manikins from going too high or too low. The four trip levers are set at a sequential 45° spacing around the shaft—at 90°, 180°, 270° and 360°—so that the left-to-right lifting pattern is 1, 2, 3, and 4.

Note how the main pivot—the 1/2-inch-diameter metal rod that runs up through the box—is distanced from the post by a 3-inch tube spacer, and is topped off with a turned finial. Finally, when you have considered all the details, sizes, and placings of all the parts that go to make up the project, sit down with graph paper, a square, a measure, and a pencil, and draw the project out to full size.

SETTING OUT THE PLYWOOD AND BUILDING THE BOX

After you have either copied the design shown here or drawn up your own modifications, transfer the various box, sail, vane, and spacer profiles through to the plywood FIG. 9-4. Double check all sizes and angles, and mark in all cutting lines and hole positions. Then use the straight saw and cut out all the profiles. Use the brace and the two bits to clear away the various holes. Rub all holes down for a smooth, easy fit. Next, glue and pin the two 3-x-3 inch square drive shaft plates either side of the front end of the box, making sure that the holes are well aligned.

Take the four cutouts that go to make up the box—the long sides and the two ends—and set them square on the workbench. Fit the front end—the end with the sails—and the two long sides together with glue and pins. When you come to fitting the back end of the box, leave out the glue and only tap the pins in enough to make a temporary hold. Have a trial dry fitting to make sure that the form is square and the various holes are well aligned (FIG. 9-6).

CUTTING THE SAIL BLOCKS AND FITTING THE BLADES

Cut the 16-inch length of 2-x-1-inch hardwood in half so that you have two pieces 8 inches long. Using the try square, carefully mark each piece of the wood off at 2 1/2 inches, 1/2 inch, 2 inches, 1/2 inch and 2 1/2 inches (FIG. 9-7). Noting that the half lap needs to be 1/2 inch deep, and the angle on the sail arm needs to be set so that the sail turns in a clockwise direction, use the straight saw and the chisels to cut and work the wood accordingly. If you are working with a 2-x-1-inch section wood, the four arms will each be angled at about 25°.

When you have cut the joint to a good crisp push-fit, smear glue on the mat-

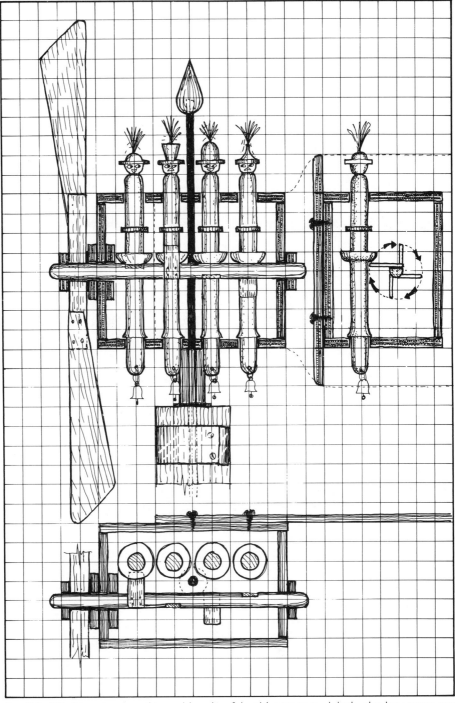

Fig. 9-2. Working drawing. At a grid scale of 1 grid square to 1 inch, the box measures about 10 × 8 × 6 inches. Note the beautiful, easy-to-make movement and the lathe-turned pieces.

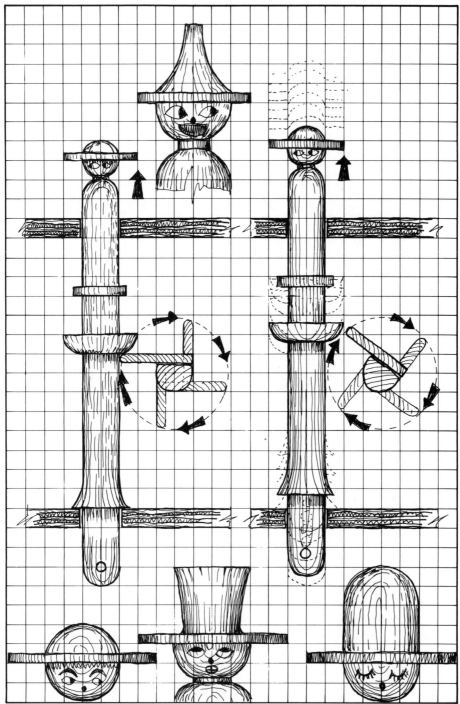

Fig. 9-3. Working drawing details. The scale is 2 grid squares to 1 inch. Study the lift-and-drop sequence of the drive shaft trip lever, and see how the turned shoulders and beads act as stops when the little figures are flipped up and down.

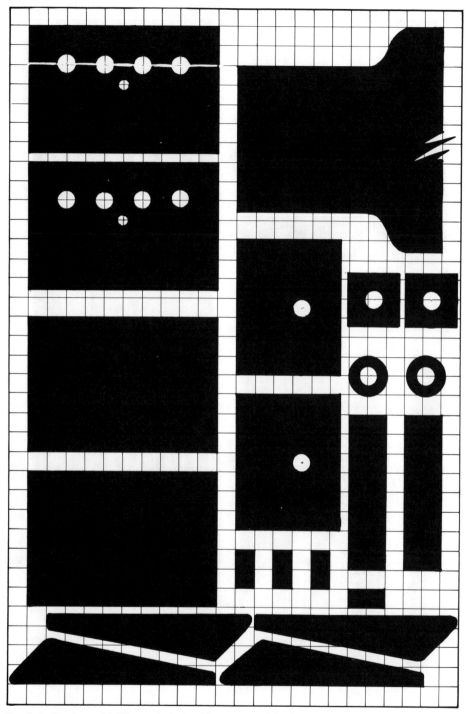

Fig. 9-4. Cutting grid. The scale is 1 grid square to 1 inch.

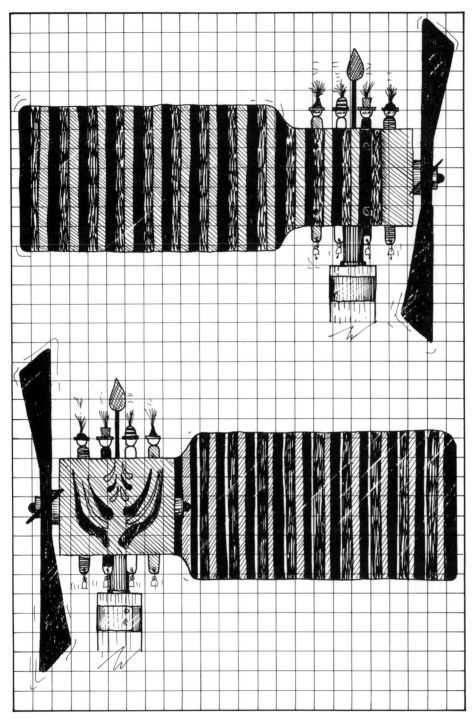

Fig. 9-5. Painting grid. An approximate scale of 2 grid squares to 3 inches.

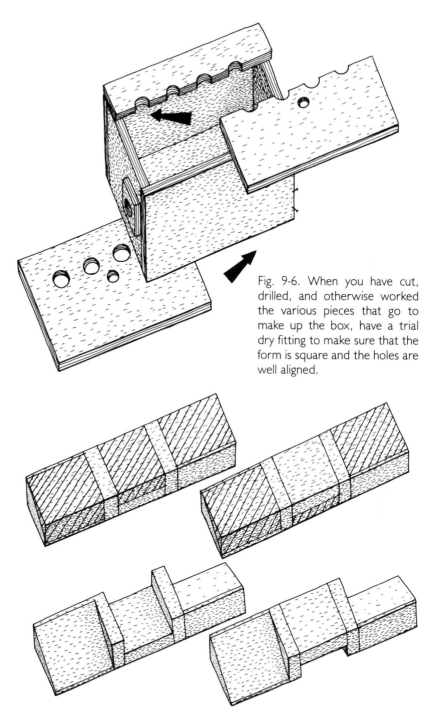

Fig. 9-6. When you have cut, drilled, and otherwise worked the various pieces that go to make up the box, have a trial dry fitting to make sure that the form is square and the holes are well aligned.

Fig. 9-7. The sail blocks. A piece at a time, carefully mark the wood off along its length at 2^1/2 inches, ^{1}/2 inch, 2 inches, ^{1}/2 inch and 2^1/2 inches. Draw in the diagonals that go to make up the design, and shade in the areas that need to be cut away.

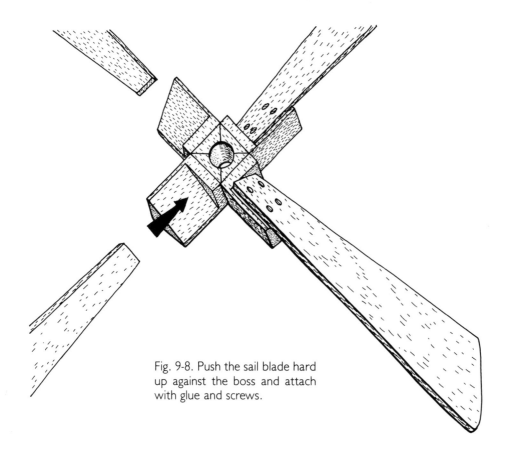

Fig. 9-8. Push the sail blade hard up against the boss and attach with glue and screws.

ing faces, slot the two pieces together, and secure the joint with a couple of brass pins. When the glue is dry, draw diagonals on the sail block boss. Establish the center and bore out a clean, loosely fitting, 1-inch-diameter hole. It's most important that the hole be square to the wood, so make sure that the drill is held at 90° to the working face (the front "cross" of the boss).

Now take the four plywood sail blades and set them out on the workbench so that the straight leading edge looks in a clockwise direction. Label each uppermost blade face "front." Then take one blade at a time and butt square on one or other of the angled faces of the sail block. Push it hard against the boss and attach it with glue and screws. Continue in this way until all four sail blades have been fitted (FIG. 9-8).

CUTTING THE SHAFT AND FITTING THE TRIP LEVERS

Re-examine the working details and see how the 1-inch-wide, 2-inch-long trip levers are positioned on the drive shaft. They are 1 inch apart and set sequentially around the shaft at 90°, 180°, 270°, and 360° or—to put it another way—at 3, 6, 9, and 12 o'clock. Set the 15-inch-long, 1-inch-diameter drive shaft out on the workbench and support it on the wooden V-blocks. Make marks from left to right

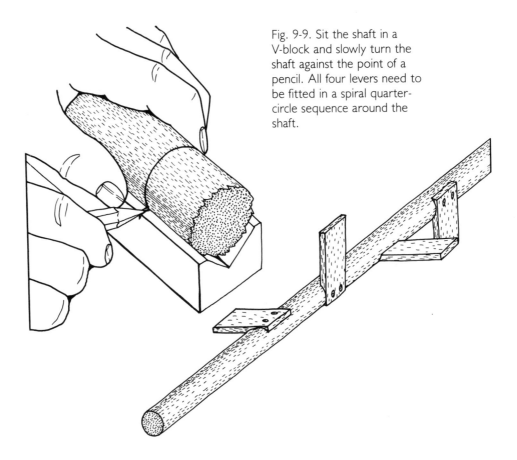

Fig. 9-9. Sit the shaft in a V-block and slowly turn the shaft against the point of a pencil. All four levers need to be fitted in a spiral quarter-circle sequence around the shaft.

along its length at 4 inches, and then at 1-inch intervals. Run the marks around the shaft by slowly revolving it up against the point of a pencil (FIG. 9-9).

Now, use a straight saw to cut either side of the first 1-inch space. Cut into the wood to a depth of about $1/4$ inch and use a chisel to clear away the waste. When you have achieved a flat, level bed or face on the lowered area, attach the first trip lever with glue and pins. When you come to fitting the second lever, turn the shaft 90°—or a quarter turn—and cut and attach as before. Continue until all four levers are fitted in a slow spiral around the shaft.

TURNING THE MANIKINS

First clear the lathe for action, making sure it is in safe working order. Keep clothing and hair tied well back out of harm's way. Cut the 2-x-2-inch wood down into four equal lengths, each at about 18 inches. Now, one piece at a time, mark off diagonals on the square cut ends. Establish center points, scribe 2-inch-diameter circles, and draw tangents on the diagonals to the circles. Now secure the wood in the vice and use the plane to clear away the corner waste. Work each length of wood until it is octagonal in section, then take off the angles until it is very nearly cylindrical.

Set the wood securely between lathe centers. Arrange all your tools so they are close at hand. Start by swiftly turning the wood down to a smooth, 2-inch-diameter cylinder. Work from left to right along the wood and, using the pencil, measure, and callipers, mark in the position of the various dips, shoulders, and beads that go to make up the manikin design. Starting from the top of the head, step off $1/2$ inch for the hat, $1/8$ inch for the brim thickness, $1/2$ inch for the face, $2^3/4$ inches down to the first stop, $1/4$ inch for the stop thickness, 1 inch between the stop and the trip ring, $1/2$ inch for the trip thickness, 4 inches between the trip and the flared stop, and finally, $2^1/2$ inches for the tail. When the marks are correctly established, switch on the lathe and cut them in with the edge of one of the tools.

Now take either a scraper or a skew chisel and clear away the between-stop waste. Turn the main body of the manikin down to a smooth, 1-inch-diameter cylinder. Note the flared area just above the bottom stop, and work the wood in the direction of the grain, from high to low. When you come to working the four curved areas—the hat, face, the curved trip ring, and the foot—aim for a smooth $1/2$-inch radius (FIG. 9-10). When you have what you consider a nicely turned form, take the graded sandpapers and rub it down to a smooth finish. Finally, part the

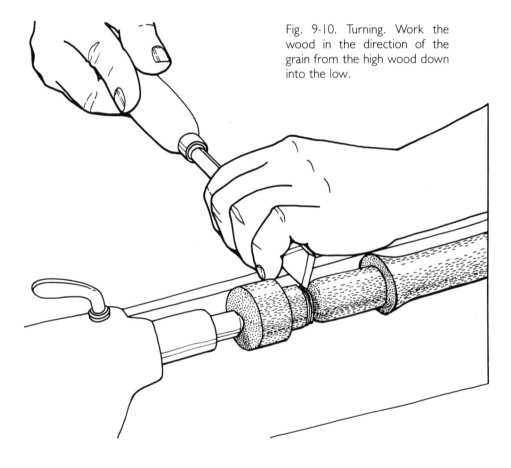

Fig. 9-10. Turning. Work the wood in the direction of the grain from the high wood down into the low.

turning off, saw off the waste, and rub the sawn ends down to a smooth round-ness. Continue until you have worked all four manikins.

ASSEMBLY

Clear the worksurface of all clutter and set out all the parts that go to make up the project: the seven pieces that make up the box, the four manikins, the shaft with the trip levers, the sail block, the tail vane, and the two shaft rings.

Carefully remove the loose end from the partially built box (the four sides). Make sure that the shaft is facing correctly, slide it into the box, pass the end of the shaft through the front hole, slide the other box side on the tail of the shaft, and attach with glue and pins. If everything is correct and the shaft is nicely pivoted in the box, carefully fit and attach the base.

Now comes the slightly tricky business of fitting and locating the manikins. One at a time, slide the manikins into the box, past the trip lever and into the base hole (FIG. 9-11). The first and second figure will be an easy fit, but fitting the last two will require some patience as you try to hold manikins 1 and 2 in place while

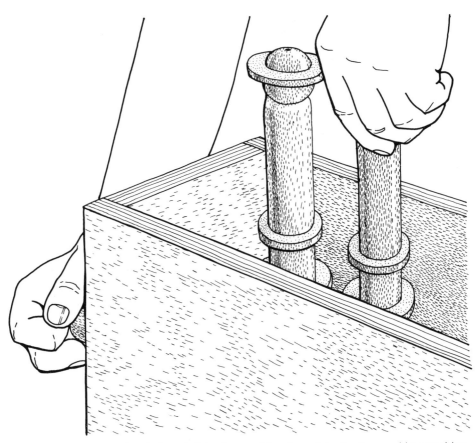

Fig. 9-11. Slowly turn the shaft and slide the manikins down into the box and into position.

turning the shaft around. You might need a little help. When all four figures are in position, slide the two halves of the box top in place and attach with pins.

After fitting thin brass washers on both ends of the shaft, slide the sail boss into position and push it against the washer and the end of the box. Now slide on both end rings and attach them to the shaft with glue and pins. Finally, position the tail vane on the side of the box and drive home the four fixing screws.

PAINTING AND FITTING

Prior to painting, rub the whole project down with the graded sandpapers, taking all corners and edges down to a rounded finish. Pay particular attention to the leading edges of the sail blades. Then clear away all the dust and debris.

Take the project to the area that you have set aside for painting. Remember to let the paint dry out between coats, and lay on a primer, two undercoats, and the ground color or topcoat. When the topcoat is dry, use a fine-point brush to pick out all the patterns, motifs, and details that go to make up the design—the little faces on the manikin dolls, the designs on the box, and the patterns on the vane (FIG. 9-5). When the paint is good and dry, lay on a couple of coats of yacht varnish.

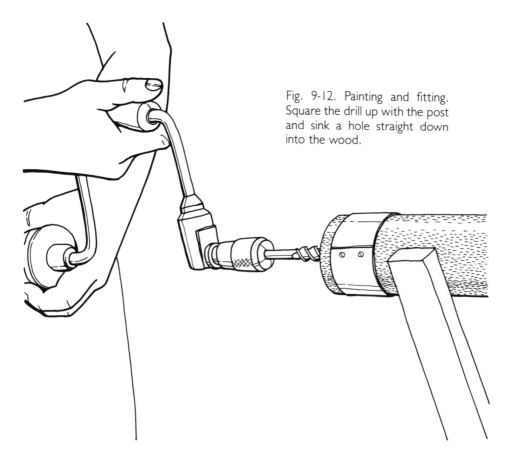

Fig. 9-12. Painting and fitting. Square the drill up with the post and sink a hole straight down into the wood.

While the varnish is drying, select a post and site for the wind machine. Choose a stout post that is about 7 feet high, with diameter between 4 and 6 inches.

Begin by binding up the top of the post with a strip of copper or a length of thin strap iron. Wrap the strapping around the post, overlap the ends, and attach with a couple of brass screws. Then locate the brace and the $1/2$-inch-diameter drill bit. Make sure the brace is held square, and sink a hole straight down into the top of the post to a depth between 6 and 7 inches (FIG. 9-12). Now file or hammer one end of the 24-inch length of $1/2$-inch-diameter rod to a rough point, and bang it into the post hole. Try to drive the rod down into the post to a depth of 8 inches. If correct, 16 inches of rod will be sticking up from the top of the post. Next, slide on the 3-inch length of tube and fit a broad washer. Smear a little grease around the rod and on top of the washer (FIG. 9-13). Carefully locate and fit the wind machine and slide on another washer. Finally, top the rod off with a turned finial, tie the bells to the bottom of the manikins, drill and fit decorative plastic topknots to their hats. The job is finished!

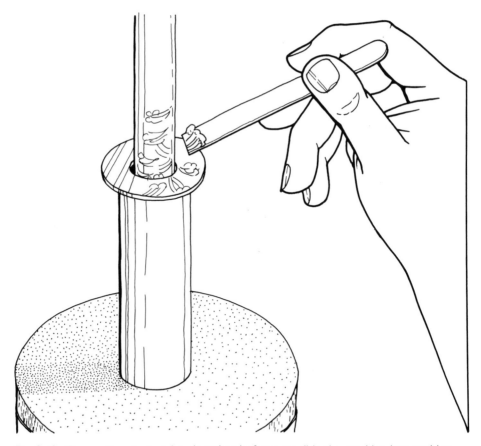

Fig. 9-13. Grease the pivot rod and washer before you slide the machine into position.

HINTS AND MODIFICATIONS

When you choose your wood—especially the wood for the turning—use a type that is straight-grained and free from knots. Ask your supplier for a good weather-resistant wood.

It is vital that the rings on the manikins be well placed and accurately turned. If you have any doubts as to the size or position of the various moving parts, build a mock-up from scrap wood and cardboard.

If you don't like the way the top of the box needs to be divided to allow it to be fitted over the manikins hats, you might modify the turning details so that the manikins hats are worked and fitted as separate units.

The 24-inch-long, $1/2$-inch-diameter metal rod needs to be a tight fit in the post and a loose fit as it passes through the box. You might need to rub out the box holes with a scrap of sandpaper or with a round file.

Bearing in mind that the machine is going to be outside in the weather, you might be able to give it some protection by fitting a roof. Perhaps you could modify the details and have the pivotal rod topped with a cone shape roof rather than a finial.

Tinkle-turn dovecote windmill

The tinkle-turn dovecote windmill is a pretty automaton. At the slightest puff of wind, the dove platform turns; and four little brass bells ring and ping (FIG. 10-1).

The project draws its inspiration from all the hundreds and thousands of tinkle-turn toys that were made in Erzgebirge, Germany, in the eighteenth and ninteenth centuries. Made of carved, turned, and painted wood, these wonderful little toys have all manner of moving figures and animals set in scenes on a box platform. The Erzgebirge carvers were very inventive: there are toys with pigeons and doves that look to be flying around a little house, scenes with people bobbing up and down, acrobats swinging, babies being rocked in their cradles, cats chasing mice, and so on. The woodcarved and whittled movements inside the boxes are ingenious. Crankshafts convert turning into a to-and-fro movement, wires and levers joined to cranks to operate jaws and limbs, and endless bands turn wheels. But better still, not only do all the toy figures move, but their movements are accompanied by tiny harp-like tinkling. When the handle or crank is turned, inside the box tiny goose quills that are set around the shaft slowly revolve and pluck at tensed wires to produce thin, high notes.

TOOLS AND MATERIALS

- [ ] A small amount of $3/8$-inch-thick multicore plywood for the doves and the four dovecote uprights
- [ ] A sheet of 1-inch-thick multicore plywood about 20×20 inches square, for the base and the small finial disc
- [ ] A sheet of $3/4$-inch-thick multicore plywood about 15 inches square, for the turntable
- [ ] A $3/8$-inch-diameter dowel about 18 inches long, for the central shaft
- [ ] Resin glue
- [ ] A $1/8$-inch-diameter nail about 2 inches long, for the pivot point
- [ ] A disc of metal or a coin $1/2$ inch in diameter, for the pivot bearing
- [ ] A wooden bead or marble for the finial ball
- [ ] Four small brass tinkle bells and a small amount of strong fishing line
- [ ] A selection of acrylic paints for the birds, colors to suit
- [ ] A roll of masking tape [ ] A can of clear yacht varnish
- [ ] A pencil and ruler [ ] A try square and beam compass

(Continued)

- ☐ A sheet each of graph paper and tracing paper
- ☐ A straight saw   ☐ A coping saw, scroll saw   ☐ A file or rasp
- ☐ A wooden V-block   ☐ A center punch and hammer
- ☐ A hand drill with bits at $1/8$ inch, $3/8$ inch, and $1/2$ inch
- ☐ A pair of pliers   ☐ A pack of graded sandpapers   ☐ A sharp knife
- ☐ A selection of broad and fine-point brushes

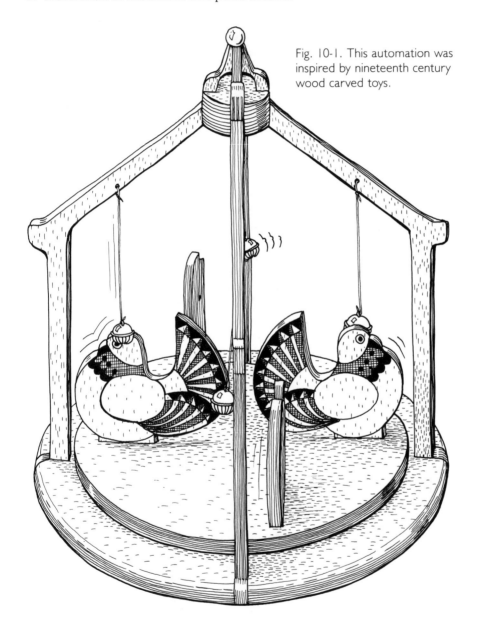

Fig. 10-1. This automation was inspired by nineteenth century wood carved toys.

DESIGN AND TECHNIQUE

Examine the working drawings (FIGS. 10-2, 10-3, and 10-4) and see how this easy-to-make project is worked and put together. Note the simple bird turntable design. See how the finial disc block collars and supports the dowel spindle, with the bottom pivot resting and turning on a very basic but extremely efficient dimple-and-point bearing.

On the front view and the plan, note how the four dove cutouts are placed, set, and mortised into the turntable to catch the wind. The doves are, in effect, both the sails and vanes. It could be said that this design is slightly faulted in that it is possible for the wind to "freeze" the action, although this is unlikely. Perhaps more to the point, this design is especially exciting in that if the wind gusts, the doves move backwards and forwards, tapping the little bells as they pass.

All in all, this design is beautifully flexible: There could be twice as many dove-shaped windvanes, and the dovecote shape could be fancier—with more curves, finials, and flourishes. If you enjoy experimenting and making modifications, then this is the project for you.

SETTING OUT AND CUTTING OUT

When you have examined the design and considered possible modifications, draw the forms to full size (FIG. 10-3), and plan the order of work. Note how the project uses at least three multicore thicknesses, with the base and the finial ring 1 inch thick, the turntable $^3/_4$ inch thick, and the four uprights and the doves $^3/_8$ inch.

When you have a clear understanding of what goes where and why, trace off the master design and pencil press transfer the traced lines through to the various thicknesses of plywood. With the cutting lines well established, label and code all the parts. Mark all mating joints—for example, you might pair up the four turntable slots and the four doves and label them 1, 2, 3, and 4. In this way, each mortise-and-tenon, or dove-to-base joint, can be individually cut and worked to fit.

When all the forms have been drawn out, set to work with saws. Rip the sheets down with the straight saw, clear away the main bulk of rough with either a bow saw or the coping saw, and cut out all the fine details with the scroll saw. To cut out the four base mortise slots, drill two $^3/_8$-inch-diameter holes—one at each end of the marked-out slots—then mount the wood in the vise and use the coping saw to join up the holes (FIG. 10-5). Finish the slots by sawing the ends square. Now take the drill and bore out the various holes.

Finally, when you have cut out all 12 bits that go to make up the design—the 11 plywood cutouts and the $^3/_8$-inch diameter dowel shaft—use the rasp, the knife, and the graded sandpapers and rub all the cut edges and surfaces down to a clean, ready-to-paint finish. Pay particular attention to the shaft holes, the mortise holes, and the tenons. Use the rasp to round off the edges of the 1-inch-thick base slab (FIG. 10-6).

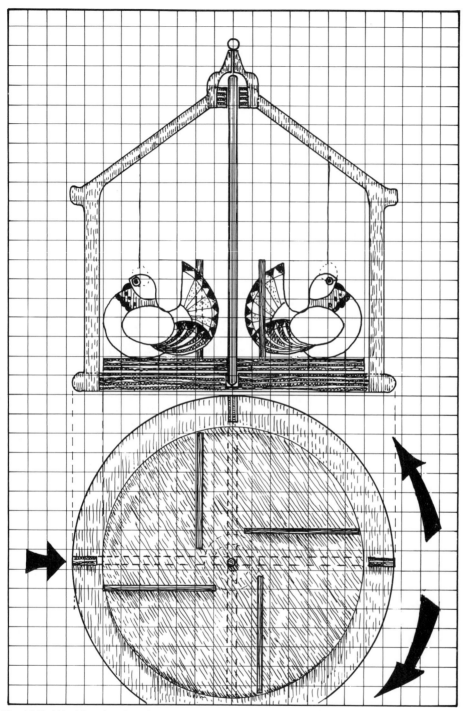

Fig. 10-2. Working drawing. At a grid scale of about 1 grid square to 1 inch, the dove cote stands about 18 – 19 inches high. Note the quartered placing of the supports and the four doves.

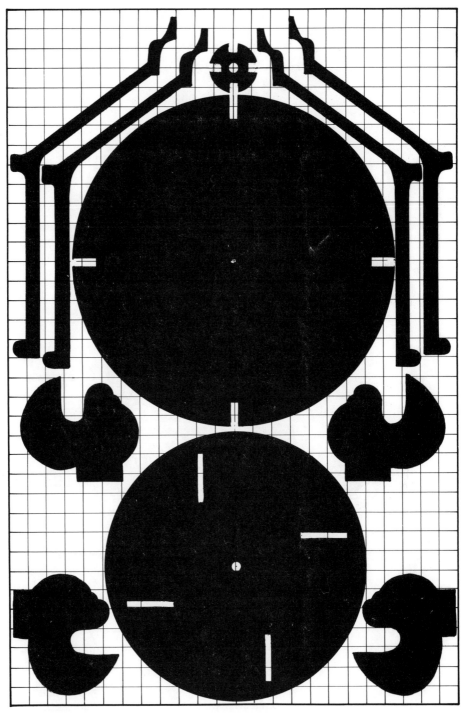

Fig. 10-3. Cutting grid. The scale is 1 grid square to 1 inch.

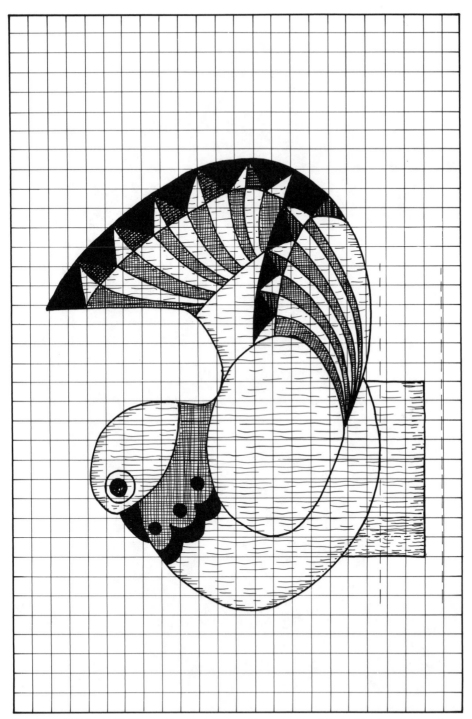

Fig. 10-4. Painting grid. The grid scale is four grid squares to 1 inch. Don't paint any fussy details, but rather go for a strong patterned folk design.

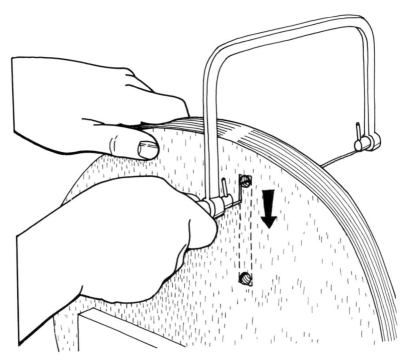

Fig. 10-5. When you have established the position of the mortise slots, drill
3/8-inch-diameter holes at the ends of the slots, then cut from hole to hole
with the coping saw.

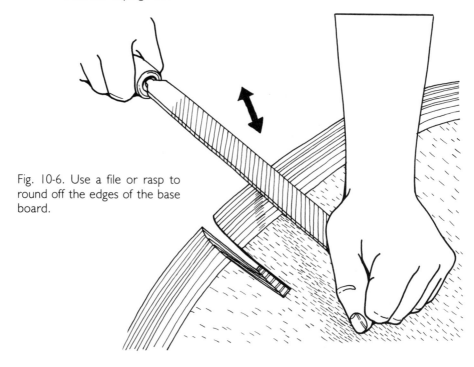

Fig. 10-6. Use a file or rasp to
round off the edges of the base
board.

FITTING THE PIVOT POINT AND THE DOVES

Take the $3/8$-inch-diameter, 18-inch-long dowel and establish the bottom pivot end. Secure the dowel in the jaws of a vise (use V-blocks), and punch a center hole. Use the hand drill and the $1/8$-inch bit, and bore a hole down into the wood to a depth of about $3/4$ inch. Don't go too deep, and make sure that you hold the drill so that the hole runs parallel to the sides of the dowel. Make a depth mark by wrapping a small tab of masking tape around the drill bit (FIG. 10-7, top).

Use a scrap of sandpaper to run the pivot end down to a round finish, then take a $1/8$-inch-diameter nail and smear its tip with a little resin glue. Push the nail into the hole and clip off its head so that there is about $1/8$ inch of nail sticking out from the end of the dowel (FIG. 10-7, bottom). Now smear a little resin glue around the center hole of the turntable and push the nail point end of the dowel down through the hole. Set it so that the point is no less than $1 1/4$ inches away from the underside of the turntable. Make sure that the dowel is at $90°$ to the top face of the turntable.

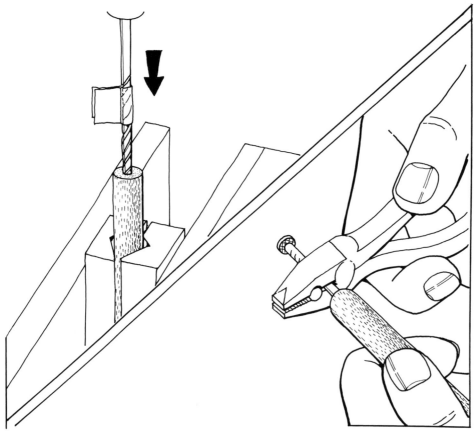

Fig. 10-7. Fitting the pivot point. With the dowel gripped in V-blocks and held in the vice, take the drill and the $1/8$-inch-diameter bit and sink a $3/4$ inch deep hole down into the dowel end (top). With the nail-pivot in place, clip off the head so as to leave a $1/8$-inch point (bottom).

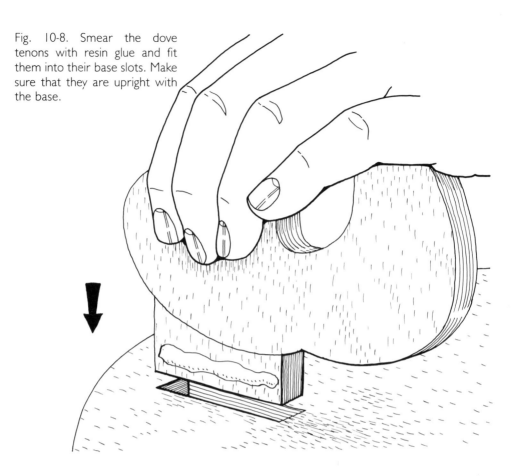

Fig. 10-8. Smear the dove tenons with resin glue and fit them into their base slots. Make sure that they are upright with the base.

Finally, take the doves and smear their base tenons with resin glue. Push them into their mortise slots so that they are set slightly back from the turntable edge and upright with the base (FIG. 10-8).

PAINTING THE DOVES

When you have achieved the turntable unit—complete with the four doves and a nail-tipped central spindle—trim off any blobs of glue, and wipe it over with a slightly dampened cloth. Then move it to the clean, dust-free area that you have set aside for painting.

Lay on an undercoat and the ground color, remembering to let the paint dry out between coats. When the paint is dry, take a tracing of the dove (FIG. 10-4) from the master design, and pencil press transfer the lines of the design through to both sides of each of the four dove cutouts. It makes it easier if you secure the tracing paper with tabs of masking tape. Lastly, take a fine-point brush and the colors of your choice, and block in all the little details that go to make up the design. Don't try to paint in any fussy naturalistic details, but rather try for bold, abstracted pattern and motifs.

ASSEMBLY

Take the four upright cutouts and the finial ring, and do a trial dry fitting. See how there is a need, when you push the uprights into the ring slots, for the leading edges at the finial top center to be mitred and cut back at 45° (FIG. 10-9). Pencil mark the corners that need to be worked, then take the rasp and sandpaper, and cut them back so that all four uprights come together for a good fit. When you are happy with the fit, smear resin glue in all four finial ring slots and slide the uprights carefully into place. When you have checked that all is correct, take an elastic band (or string or sticky tape), and strap the finial top up until the glue is set (FIG. 10-10).

Now, take the base—the large, 1-inch-thick disc—and punch in the center point. Use the hand drill and the 1/2-inch-diameter bit to sink a 3/4-inch-deep hole. Take your 1/2-inch-diameter metal disc, which might be a coin or some sort of blank, and punch it in the middle to make a dimple. Smear the dimple with oil and drop it in the hole (FIG. 10-11).

On the large top-like turntable, locate the nail point pivot end of the dowel in the base hole and on the punched metal bearing. Having trimmed the top end of the dowel to a good fit and length, carefully slide the finial ring over the dowel and lower the four-legged cage into position. Smear resin glue over each "foot"

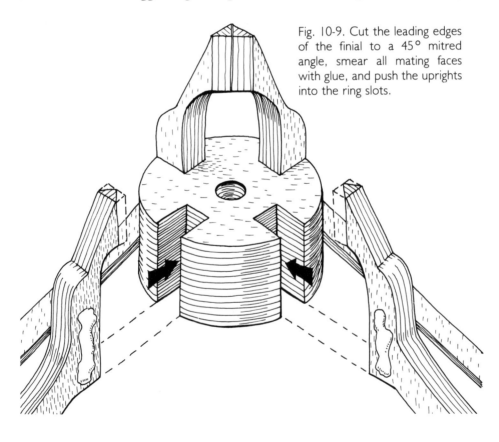

Fig. 10-9. Cut the leading edges of the finial to a 45° mitred angle, smear all mating faces with glue, and push the uprights into the ring slots.

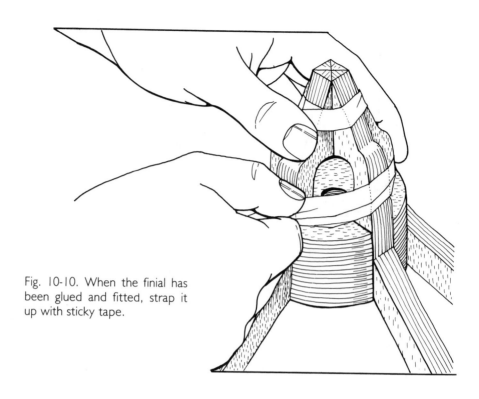

Fig. 10-10. When the finial has been glued and fitted, strap it up with sticky tape.

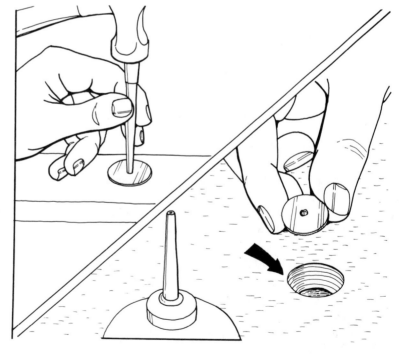

Fig. 10-11. Assembly. Punch the $1/2$-inch-diameter disc to make a dent or dimple bearing point (top). Drop the metal disc into the hole and oil the dimple (bottom).

Fig. 10-12. Glue the feet and put them into their base rim slots.

and, while making sure the other legs aren't being wrenched or twisted, carefully locate the foot in the base rim slot (FIG. 10-12).

Take a few small pins and bang them at an angle well into the joint. Glue a marble or bead on top of the finial mount. Rub the various joints down with graded sandpaper and make sure the feet run smoothly into the base profile. Lay on several coats of varnish. Finally, hang the four bells from the roof so that they can be knocked by the doves. Position the whole workpiece in a breezy corner of the garden and sit back and enjoy the action.

HINTS AND MODIFICATIONS

If you have doubts about the way the doves are set to catch the wind—that is, the angle the doves are set on the turntable—you could experiment with a cardboard mock-up and make changes.

You can reduce the friction at the bearings by waxing the top of the shaft and making sure that the bottom of the dowel doesn't rub on the base hole.

Pecking bird whirligig

This whirligig was inspired by an American "pecking turkey" toy, a beautiful woodcarved and painted pendulum toy thought to have been made in Pennsylvania about the middle of the nineteenth century. It is easy to make, very attractive, ingenious in its movement, and good fun (FIG. 11-1)

The lifelike movement of the bird is really very clever. When the wind catches the sail, the mainshaft turns, the trip lever cam flicks the hanging pendulum, the pendulum bob swings into motion, and the bird—very realistically—looks to be pecking up food. Set this whirligig up outside your window and it will give you hours of delight.

TOOLS AND MATERIALS

☐ A sheet of $^1/_2$-inch-thick multicore plywood for the five box sides, the two stop rings, the two trip lever cams, and the pendulum bob

☐ A sheet of $^3/_8$-inch-thick multicore plywood for the five pieces that go to make up the bird and the tail vane

☐ A 20-inch length of $^3/_4$-inch-diameter broomstick dowel for the drive shaft

☐ A 20-inch length of 1-inch-diameter broomstick dowel for the pivotal shaft

☐ A 20-inch length of 2-×-1$^1/_2$-inch wood for the sail propeller. An easy-to-work, straight-grained wood like lime or white pine is best

☐ A 4-inch length of coathanger wire for the two bird pivot rods

☐ Eight brass washers to fit the coathanger wire

☐ A length of fine twine for the pendulum cord

☐ A handful of $^3/_4$-inch-long panel pins/nails for the box. Brass ovals are best

☐ A can or tube of waterproof wood glue

☐ Acrylic paints, colors to suit   ☐ A can of clear yacht varnish

☐ A large sheet each of graph paper and tracing paper

☐ A try square   ☐ A pencil and measure

☐ A straight saw   ☐ A coping saw

☐ A hand drill with drill bits at 1 inch, $^3/_4$ inch, $^1/_2$ inch, and $^1/_4$ inch

☐ A few chisels—$^1/_4$ inch and $^1/_2$ inch

☐ A hammer and a mallet

☐ A handknife. A large, sharp-bladed clasp knife works best

(Continued)

□ A pack of graded sandpapers □ A selection of paint brushes
□ General workshop tools and material

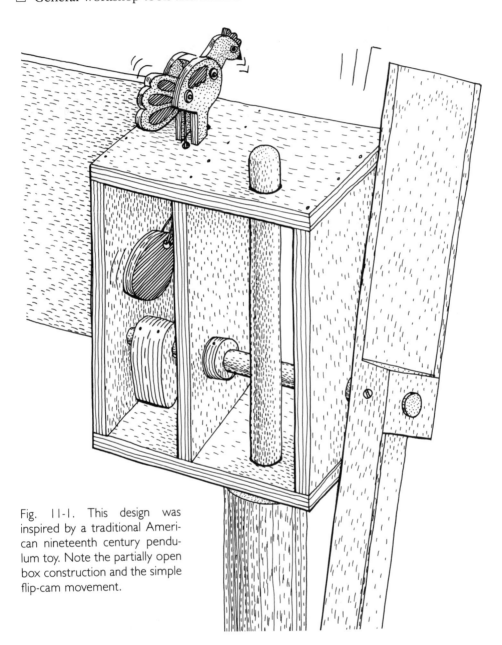

Fig. 11-1. This design was inspired by a traditional American nineteenth century pendulum toy. Note the partially open box construction and the simple flip-cam movement.

DESIGN AND TECHNIQUE

Examine the working drawings (FIGS. 11-2, 11-3, and 11-4), and see how the machine is made and put together. The project is made up from two different plywood

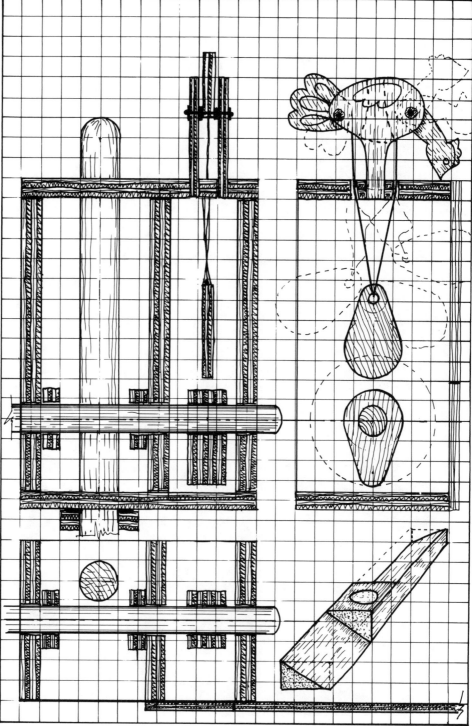

Fig. 11-2. Working drawing. At a grid scale of 2 grid squares to 1 inch, the box measures about 6 × 8 × 4 inches. Note: The little sail block detail in the bottom right hand corner is not to scale.

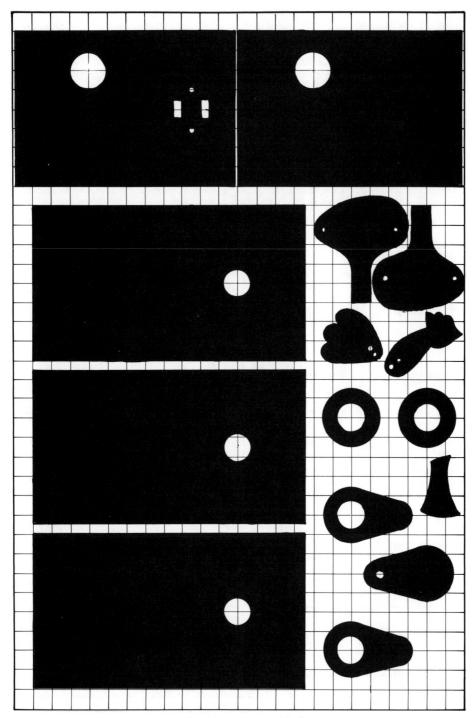

Fig. 11-3. Cutting grid. The scale is 2 grid squares to 1 inch.

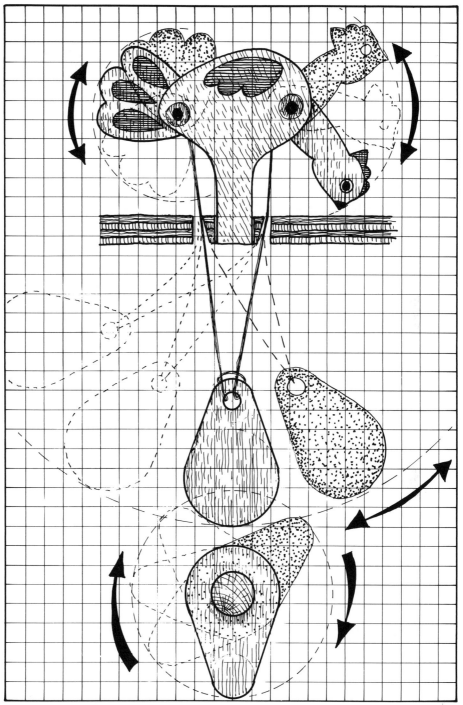

Fig. 11-4. Working drawing and painting grid. The scale is approximately 4 grid squares to 1 inch. Note how the revolving cam flips the pendulum and sets the little bird into motion.

thicknesses, the trip lever cam is fitted on the drive shaft, and the sail propeller is cut and carved from a single length of 2-x-1$\frac{1}{2}$-inch wood. Note how the traditional bird toy is fitted into mortise slots on top of the box and how it is worked by a swinging pendulum. The working action is beautifully simple: the wind hits and turns the sail propeller, the drive shaft turns around, the fixed cam on the drive shaft hits the pendulum bob, and the pendulum bob swings and sets the bird's head and tail rocking on pivots. An added design feature is that the workings can be seen through the open sides of the box.

CUTTING, DRILLING, AND SANDING

When you have studied the working details, sorted out what goes where, draw the flatwood parts out to full size (FIG. 11-3). Make tracings and pencil press transfer the traced lines through to the working face of the plywood (FIG. 11-5). Bear in mind that the box sides and the various rings need to be worked in $\frac{1}{2}$-inch-thick wood, while the bird and the vane are best worked from slightly thinner $\frac{3}{8}$-inch-thick material.

Fig. 11-5. Draw the parts out to full size, take a tracing, and then pencil press transfer the traced lines through to the working face of the wood. Note that the bird and the vane are worked from $\frac{3}{8}$-inch-thick materials.

Check out all the sizes and details and mark and label the pieces so as to avoid mix-ups. Then use the straight saw, the coping saw, and the drills to cut and work all the forms that go to make up the design. Use the graded sandpapers to rub all the cut edges down to a smooth finish. Finally, rub the edges of the 3/4-inch and 1-inch shaft holes down so that they are slightly over size. This will ensure that the shafts are an easy smooth fit.

BUILDING THE BOX AND FITTING THE DRIVE SHAFT

When you have worked all the pieces that go to make up the project, take the base board, pencil, ruler, and square, and mark in the position of the three upright panels. Check the placing, and, one piece at a time, glue the bottom of each panel and nail pin through, from the base. Turn the half-built box right-side up, and set it down on the worksurface so that the head end (the sail propeller end) is facing left. Now pass the 3/4-inch-diameter dowel from left to right—through the box end, the two stop rings, the middle partition, the two trip lever cams, and on out through the right hand end of the box (FIG. 11-6).

Fig. 11-6. Pass the 3/4-inch-diameter dowel through the partially built box. From left to right, pass the dowel through: the box end, the two stop rings, the middle partition, and on through the two trip cams and the right hand end of the box.

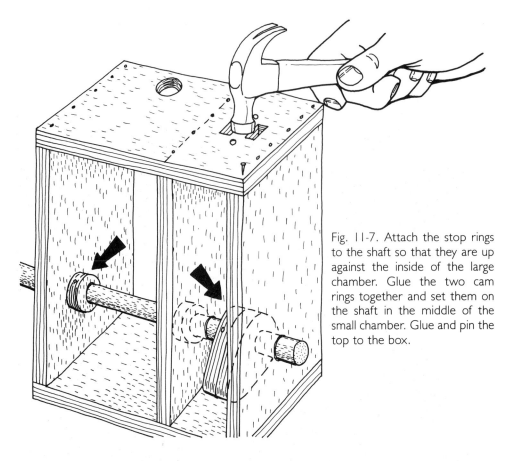

Fig. 11-7. Attach the stop rings to the shaft so that they are up against the inside of the large chamber. Glue the two cam rings together and set them on the shaft in the middle of the small chamber. Glue and pin the top to the box.

With about 1 inch of the shaft sticking out through the tail vane end of the box, slide the two stop rings apart until they are a loose fit up against the inside of the large chamber, and attach them to the shaft with glue and pins. Now slide the two trip lever cam rings together, smear their mating faces with a little glue, and attach them so that they are set in the middle of the box cavity (FIG. 11-7). Finally, when you have glued and pinned the top to the box, put it to one side until the glue has set.

FITTING, PAINTING, AND FIXING THE BIRD

The bird is made of $^3/_8$-inch-thick ply. Take the three pieces that go to make the body—the two body halves and the spacer—and glue and pin them together to make a total body thickness of $1^1/_8$ inches. Before you go any further, do a trial dry run assembly to make sure everything fits well. Take the two 2-inch lengths of coathanger wire and the washers, and pivot the head and the tail inside the body cavity. Make sure that they see-saw freely on their pivots and that the pendulum string holes are well placed (FIG. 11-8, bottom left).

When the overall fit is correct, dismantle the bird and rub it down with the graded sandpapers until the wood is smooth to the touch. Now you can begin

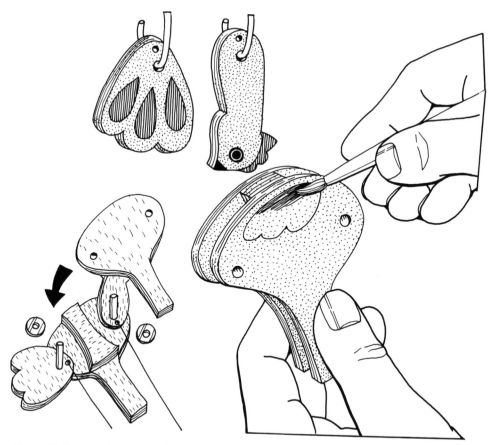

Fig. 11-8. Painting. When you have glued and pinned the three parts that go to make up the body of the bird, check that the pendulum string holes are correctly placed (bottom left). Having worked out how the parts are going to be supported while they are wet, take a fine point brush and lay on all the coats of paint that go to make up the design (top right).

painting, which is best done in a dust-free area. On the head, tail, and body, lay on the coats of paint that go to make up the design: the undercoat, the topcoat, and all the feather, eye, and tail details (FIG. 11-8). It's a good idea to suspend the drying pieces from wire loops threaded through the pivot holes.

When the paint is dry, check that the pivot and string holes are clean and open. Smear a little glue on the bird's feet—that is, over the tenons—and set them squarely in the two mortise slots on top of the box. Then knot the two lengths of fine, strong cord or twine onto the head and tail and pass them down through the pendulum holes on top of the box. Make sure that there are four washers on each pivot—one at the start and one at the finish—and washers between wood layers. Refit the bird's head and tail, and slide home the wire pivots. Nip and deform the pivot ends with a pair of pliers, and clip off the waste (FIG. 11-9). Finally, tie on the pendulum bob and adjust the strings so that, in turning, the trip lever just strikes the bob.

Fig. 11-9. Painting and attaching. Pass the pivot wires through the various washers and moving parts, deform the pivot ends, and clip off the waste.

CUTTING, CARVING, AND FITTING THE SAIL PROPELLER

Check the 20-inch-long piece of 20-x-1¹/₂-inch wood to make sure that it is free from knots, splits, cracks, and stains. With pencil, ruler, and square, mark the wood off along its length at 9 inches, 2 inches, 9 inches (FIG. 11-10). Run diagonal lines across the 2-x-2-inch square to fix the center, and use the drill and the ³/₄-inch-diameter bit to bore out the drive shaft hole. One end at a time, draw diagonals that run down from left to right. Make a diagonal saw cut down each side of the 2-x-2-inch central section and then, with chisel and knife, cut in from the end grain. Don't try to remove the waste in one great chop—take it off in thin slices.

When you have the basic propeller shape, use the graded sandpapers to rub all the faces and sharp edges down to a smooth rounded finish. Then take the drill and the ³/₄-inch bit and bore out the drive shaft hole. Finally, set the propeller on the end of the drive shaft and attach it with a brass screw (FIG. 11-11).

FINISHING

Examine FIG. 11-2 and note that the propeller direction isn't important. It can turn clockwise or counter-clockwise, as long as the trip lever strikes the pendulum bob

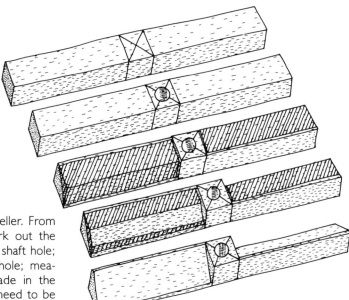

Fig. 11-10. The propeller. From top to bottom, mark out the position of the drive shaft hole; bore out the shaft hole; measure, mark, and shade in the areas of waste that need to be cut away; use a chisel and a knife to cut away the waste; rub the wood down to a good finish.

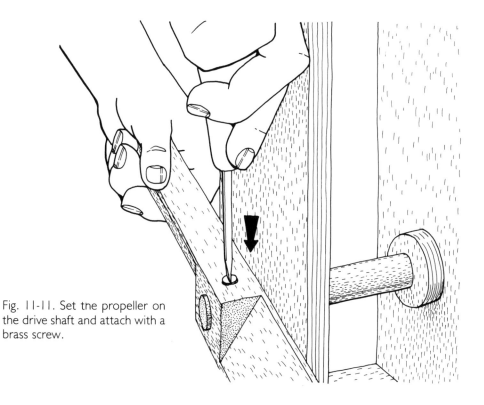

Fig. 11-11. Set the propeller on the drive shaft and attach with a brass screw.

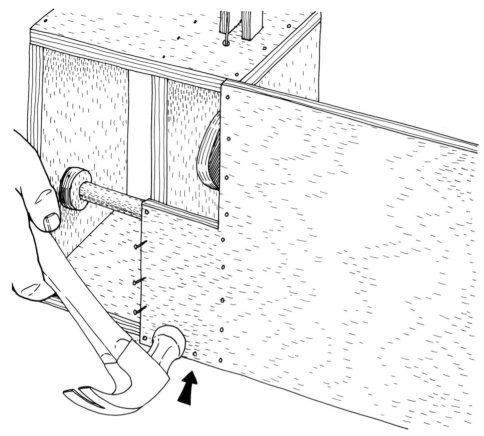

Fig. 11-12. Cut and fit a small tail vane and fit it to the box so that the pendulum can swing freely.

and the pendulum can swing freely. The tail rudder needs to be long only if you want the propeller to turn into the wind. Cut and fit a small vane about 8×10 inches (FIG. 11-12). Rub down all the rough edges and lay on a couple of coats of clear yacht varnish. Finally, bore out the top of the mounting post with a 1-inch-diameter hole, and hammer home the 1-inch-diameter main pivot dowel. Slide on the stop ring and a metal or plastic washer, set the machine in place on the pivot, and the job is done.

HINTS AND MODIFICATIONS

If you want an all-wood machine, you could replace the wire pivots and the screws with hardwood dowels and pegs. If the machine is to be exposed to all weathers, make sure that the drive holes be loose fitting. Protect the wood with at least two coats of yacht varnish—pay particular attention to the ply edges and the drive shafts.

When you are choosing wood for the propeller, make sure that it's easy to work, straight-grained, and free from dead knots, splits, warps and sappy edges.

Merry-go-round windmill

Most of use have, at some time or other, had a ride on a traditional merry-go-round, or fairground carousel. Huge woodcarved horses, all brilliantly painted and going up and down, and round and round—what fun! The gold painted signs, bright brass barleytwist metalwork, mirrors, flashing colored lights, and loud steam organ music, inspire memories of "the fun of the fair."

This wind machine is a real dazzler. It is a charming, quiet windmill that draws its inspirations from traditional carousel horses—one that is brightly painted and altogether beautiful (FIG. 12-1).

TOOLS AND MATERIALS

- [ ] A quantity of $1/4$-inch-thick multicore plywood for the six wind vanes, the six-slotted wind vane disc, the three-slotted horse disc, and the three horses
- [ ] A quantity of $1/2$-inch-thick multicore plywood for the top disc—which is the disc that goes over the horses and is carried by three poles
- [ ] A quantity of 1-inch-thick multicore plywood for the base disc
- [ ] A 24-inch length of $1/2$-inch-diameter dowel for the three barleytwist poles
- [ ] A 14-inch length of $3/8$-inch-diameter dowel for the main central drive shaft
- [ ] A large wooden ball or shaped turning for the decorative shaft finial
- [ ] A $3/8$-inch-diameter steel ball bearing to drop in the central base shaft hole
- [ ] Resin glue   [ ] A roll of masking tape
- [ ] A good selection of odds and ends of wood, to be used when gluing up
- [ ] Acrylic paint, colors to suit   [ ] A can of yacht varnish
- [ ] Several large sheets each of graph paper and tracing paper
- [ ] A pencil and ruler   [ ] A beam compass and try square
- [ ] A straight saw   [ ] A coping saw or scroll saw   [ ] A rasp
- [ ] A pack of graded sandpapers
- [ ] A hand drill with bits at $3/4$ inch, $1/2$ inch, and $3/8$ inch
- [ ] A good selection of broad and fine-point paint brushes
- [ ] Cloths, newspaper, string, and masking tape

Fig. 12-1. This is a merry-go-round windmill in the nineteenth century carousel tradition. Note that the six tent-like vanes and the three horses are all designed to catch the wind.

DESIGN AND TECHNIQUE

Examine the working drawing details (FIG. 12-2), and note how the windmill is layered and built up using discs and dowels. The project uses compass radius step-offs to subdivide circles in order to establish the various positions of the horses and the wind vanes. The whole top of the carousel is made up of six vanes that directly turn the central shaft and the horse turntable. Because the three horses are set on the same axis as the vanes, they also act as wind sails. Notice the way the shaft turns on a ball bearing, and how the whole merry-go-round is brightly painted, with the support poles given spiral lines and colors to create a realistic barleytwist effect.

The slotted construction means that the project can be made using a minimum of tools and a few basic building techniques. One of the instruments used

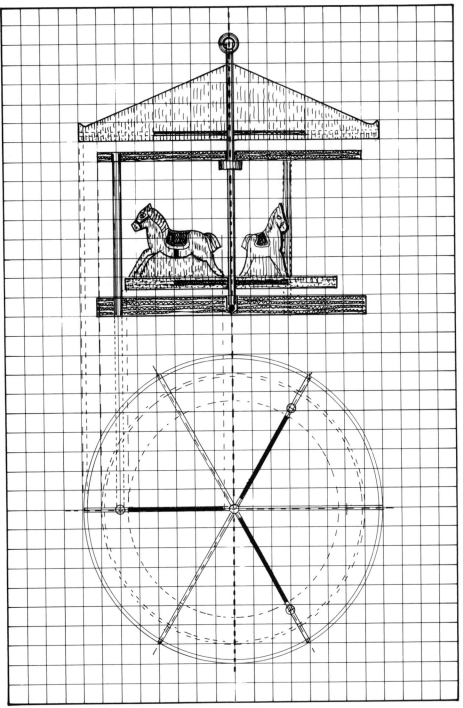

Fig. 12-2. Working drawing. At a grid scale of about 1 grid square to 1 inch, the carousel is 14 inches in diameter and 14–15 inches high. See how the whole design is based on divided circles.

here—the beam compass—can quickly be made with a strip of wood, a screw, and a pencil (refer to FIG. 12-7).

SETTING OUT THE DESIGN

When you have spent time looking at the design and you have a clear understanding of how the project needs to be worked and put together, use a pencil, ruler, beam compass, and set-square to draw the various forms to full size (FIGS. 12-3, 12-4, and 12-5). The project uses three thicknesses of sheet wood: $1/4$-inch ply for the two moving discs, $1/2$-inch ply for the top, and 1-inch ply for the base.

When you have finalized all the forms and details, take a tracing and pencil press transfer the traced lines through to working faces of the various pieces of wood. Make sure that all the lines are well established and label the forms so you know exactly where they fit in relationship to each other. Use the coping saw or scroll saw and cut out the forms. When you are cutting out the discs, cut well to the outside of the drawn lines and then finish by cutting back to the line with a rasp and sandpaper (FIG. 12-6).

Using compass, ruler, and pencil set out the equally spaced center-to-side lines on the discs. Establish the center point of each disc, set the compass to the radius measurement, and then step off scribing arcs (FIG. 12-7). Draw straight lines from the circumference/arc crosses through to the center. The whole project relates to the hexamerous six-point the grid: the top wind vane uses all six lines, the horses use alternate lines, the three poles are spaced on the lines, and so on (FIG. 12-2).

Finally, use the coping saw to cut out all the slots that go to make up the design.

FITTING THE SUPPORT POLES AND THE MAIN BEARING

Set the 1-inch-thick base disc and the $1/2$-inch top disc out on the worksurface and establish the position of the various holes. Start with the support pole holes (which are later painted to give a barleytwist effect), and fix their position by measuring 6 inches out from the center point—out along all three spaced radius lines. Then drill holes through the wood thickness using the $1/2$-inch-diameter bit. When drilling out the $1/2$-inch-diameter center hole in the 1-inch base slab, be careful that you *do not* run the drill through the wood thickness. Examine the working drawing details in FIG. 12-2 and see how the $3/8$-inch-diameter ball bearing needs to sit in the bottom of the hole.

Finally, saw the 24-inch length of $1/2$-inch-diameter dowel into three 8-inch pieces. Fit them into their post holes. Don't worry about the poles being wobbly at this stage, just make sure that they are all the same length and that the structure is able to sit square (FIG. 12-8).

MAKING THE MAIN SAIL VANE

Set the main shaft, the six wind vanes, and the top disc out on the worksurface. Start by running a $3/8$-inch-diameter hole through the center of the disc. Have a

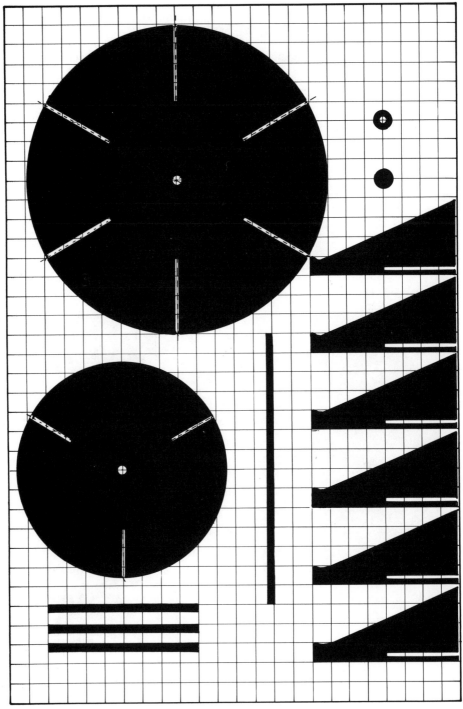

Fig. 12-3. Cutting grid. The scale is 1 grid square to 1 inch.

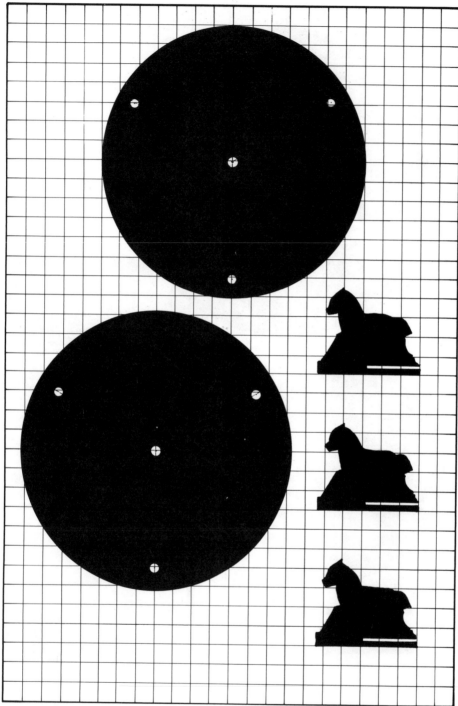

Fig. 12-4. Cutting grid. The scale is 1 grid square to 1 inch.

Fig. 12-5. Painting grid. The scale is approximately 2 grid squares to 1 inch. Note the bold imagery. Use bold colors and large areas of pattern.

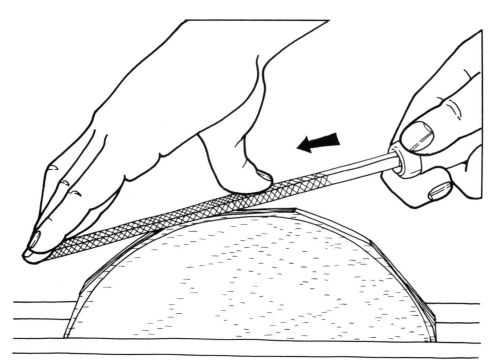

Fig. 12-6. When you have cut out the discs—that is, with the line of cut being well to the waste side of the drawn lines, cut back to the line with a rasp and sandpaper.

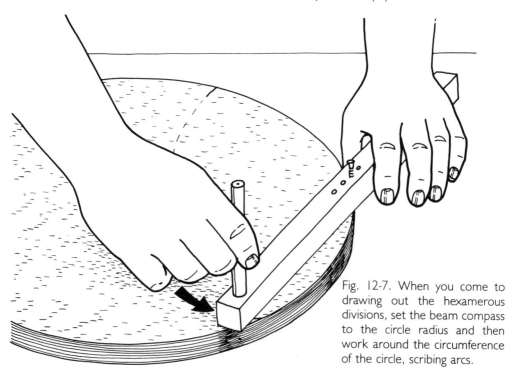

Fig. 12-7. When you come to drawing out the hexamerous divisions, set the beam compass to the circle radius and then work around the circumference of the circle, scribing arcs.

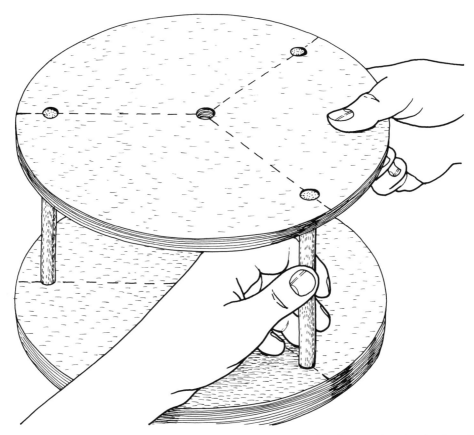

Fig. 12-8. Dry-fit the poles into the top and bottom holes and make sure that the structure is able to sit square and stable.

trial dry fitting with the dowel and the six vanes. Pass the dowel through the center hole and then, one piece at a time, slot and slide the vanes into position on the disc. Push the wedge-shaped vanes along their slots until they are set hard up against the dowel shaft, and so that the short wedge side/ends sit flush with the side of the disc (FIG. 12-9). If one or other of the wedges fails to butt up against the shaft, adjust the slots to fit. With about $8^{1}/2$inches of shaft sticking up through the topside of the disc, smear resin glue on all mating faces of shaft, disc, and vanes, and set the vanes upright. Finally, stick the finial ball on top of the shaft and put the whole umbrella-like construction carefully to one side until the glue is set.

MAKING THE HORSE TURNTABLE

Set the three horse cutouts and the turntable disc (which has three slots) out on the worksurface. Once you have drilled out the $^{3}/_{8}$-inch-diameter central hole, take your horse tracing and a hard pencil, and press the horse imagery through to both sides of all three cutouts. Now—just as you did with the wind vanes—cut, fit, and slide the horses into position along their slots so that they are set at 90° to

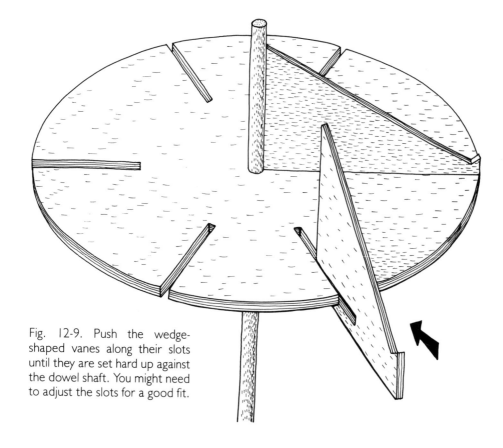

Fig. 12-9. Push the wedge-shaped vanes along their slots until they are set hard up against the dowel shaft. You might need to adjust the slots for a good fit.

the turntable and so that they are able to butt hard up against the central shaft. When you have made sure that the leading edge of each horse is trimmed flush with the edge of the disc, smear the slots with glue and set the horses in position (FIG. 12-10).

ASSEMBLY

When you have worked all the parts that go to make up the design, clear the worksurface of all clutter and be ready with the resin glue. With the base set face-up on the bench, dab glue in all six pole holes (base and top), and set the three 8-inch dowels and the top disc carefully into position. Now, pop the steel ball and a dab of grease in the bearing hole, and arrange the turntable in position on the base. Pass the shaft of the umbrella-like unit down through the central hole. Slide the ring on the shaft, then continue passing the shaft down through the turntable and on into the ball bearing hole (FIG. 12-11).

Finally, when the whole workpiece has been positioned and glued—so that the turntable is set up from the base; the ring is just clear of the underside of the roof; and the horses, poles, top and shaft all look to be true, square, and upright—strap, wedge, and otherwise secure the structure until the glue is set (FIG. 12-12).

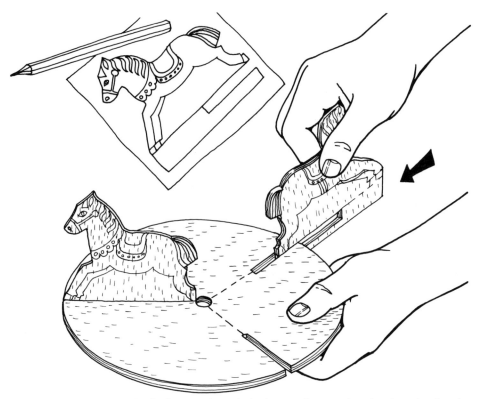

Fig. 12-10. When you slide the horses along their slots, make sure that they butt hard against the central shaft and stand upright at right angles to the turntable.

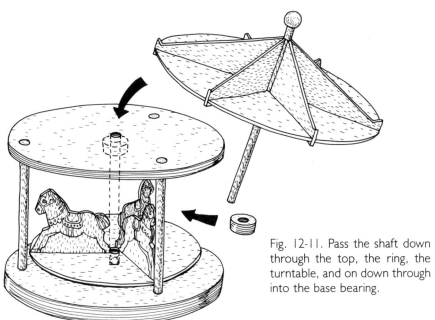

Fig. 12-11. Pass the shaft down through the top, the ring, the turntable, and on down through into the base bearing.

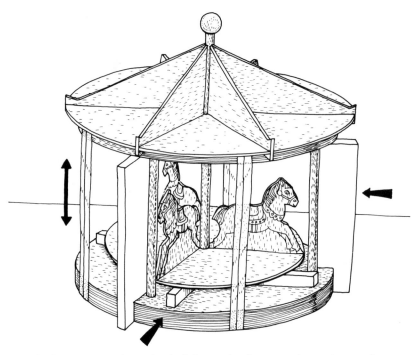

Fig. 12-12. When you have glued all the mating faces, wedge and strap the structure so that it is square and stable.

PAINTING

When the glue is set, make sure that the turning action of the wind vane and roundabout is smooth and easy. Then take a knife and a scrap of sandpaper and carefully go over the project. Trim and rub down the whole piece; make sure it is free from hard glue blobs, splinters, and sharp edges. When you have a smooth, ready-to-paint finish, use a slightly damp cloth to remove all the wood dust. Arrange the piece in the area that you have set aside for painting.

Starting with the most inaccessible corners and surfaces, work up, out, and over, all the while laying on the main blocks of color. For example, you might first paint the underside of the base, then the underside of the top, then the central shaft, and so on. When the large areas of ground color are dry, use a fine brush to pick out all the dots, dashes, and daubs that go to make up the design (see FIG. 12-5).

Use strong primary colors. You might paint the wind vane a bright red, the shaft bright blue, the horse white, the turntable disc and the barleytwist poles a yellow, and so on. Aim for strong patterns, picking out the details with contrasting colors of black, gold, sharp yellow, and green. Continue laying on smaller and smaller details, one on top of another. When you have achieved a striking effect, lay on at least two coats of clear varnish and set the project out in the sun to dry.

Screw fix the base out in the garden—perhaps on a post by the gate—and then sit back and watch the fun.

HINTS AND MODIFICATIONS

Bearing in mind that the six wind vanes and the three horses are set on their discs in identical order, you might adjust the design so that there are an equal number of vanes to horses—six vanes and six horses, or three vanes and three horses.

Because this project is difficult to paint, you might paint the cutout parts before you put them together and touch up any damaged areas after assembly. You could try for a different effect by laying on a varnished ground and then only using the colors for the decorative details.

Assembly is both tricky and sticky; speed up the process by using a hot glue gun. You could make things easier by letting the glue set between stages. Glue the vanes first, then the horse to the turntable, then the turntable to the shaft, and so on.

13
Fisherman windmill

The fisherman windmill is one of my favorites. This poor old boy spends all his time heaving and casting, heaving and casting—little knowing that he is not the hunter but the hunted. He is about to be snapped up by "Moby Dick" (FIG. 13-1).

This particular automaton beautifully illustrates the delightful, jokey, pleasuresome possibilities of whirligig making. And of course the imagery can be modified to suit just about any activity that you care to think of. The man could be clutching a shotgun and the tail vane worked in the form of a fearsome cougar. Then again, the figure could be skiing, playing golf, dancing, or walking a dog. If you do want to change the design, then you must take into account the rotating direction of the shaft and the sweep of the trip lever. And the fish on the end of the line isn't only ornamental, it is a necessary counterbalance, so take this into consideration when modifying the design.

The movement is straight forward: The mainshaft turns, the sweeping trip lever comes into contact with the hooked extension, the man tilts backwards, the trip lever moves on through its arc, and the weighted fish pulls the man back upright.

TOOLS AND MATERIALS

☐ A sheet of 3/8-inch-thick, multicore plywood 48 inches long and 24 inches wide, for the sides of the box, the pieces that go to make up the fisherman, and the two sails and the vane
☐ A 1-inch-diameter dowel about 12 inches long for the main drive shaft
☐ A 1/2-inch-diameter steel rod about 18 inches long for the box-to-post pivotal rod
☐ A piece of prepared 2-x-1-inch hardwood 10 inches long for the sail blocks
☐ A sheet of cardboard
☐ One 2-inch brass split pin with four brass washers to fit
☐ A couple of large brass washers to fit the 1/2-inch pivotal rod
☐ A handful of 3/4-inch-long brass panel pins for assembly
☐ A roll of galvanized wire for the fishing rod and the post binding
☐ A couple of large fencing staples
☐ A length of fine brass picture wire for the fishing line
☐ About 12, 3/4-inch brass screws for the sails and vane
☐ Waterproof glue   ☐ Enamel paints, colors to suit
☐ A can of yacht varnish
☐ A large sheet each of graph paper and tracing paper
☐ A pencil and measure   ☐ A pair of scissors   ☐ A try square

(Continued)

☐ A compass ☐ A ³/₈-inch-wide chisel ☐ A mallet
☐ A coping saw ☐ A small straight saw
☐ A hand drill with a good selection of drill bits
☐ A pair of pliers ☐ A hammer ☐ A rasp
☐ A pack of graded sandpapers
☐ A couple of paint brushes, one broad and one fine-point

Fig. 13-1. Here is a fun whirligig classic.

DESIGN AND TECHNIQUE

Examine the working drawings (FIGS. 13-2, 13-3, and 13-4) and note how the project comes together and how the movement works: the simple sweeping action of the

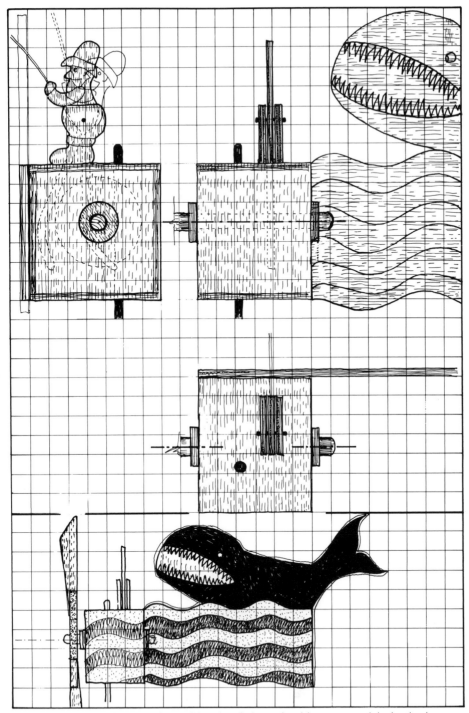

Fig. 13-2. Working drawing. At a grid scale of about 1 grid square to 1 inch, the box measures 6 × 7 × 7 inches, and the fisherman figure stands about 6 – 7 inches high (top). The scale is about 1 grid square to 2 inches.

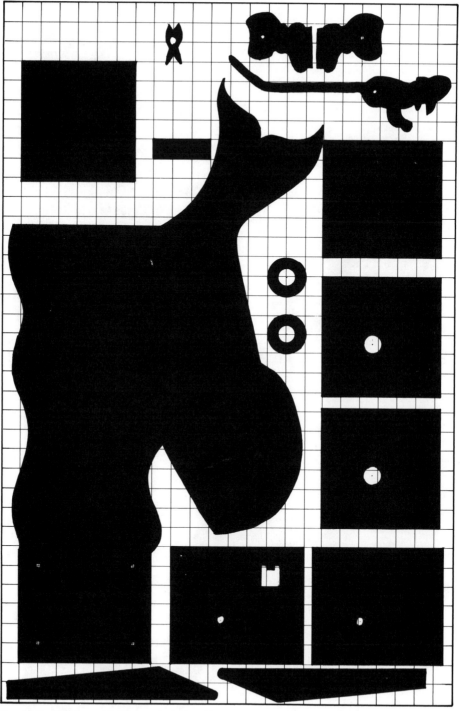

Fig. 13-3. Cutting grid. The scale is 1 grid square to 1 inch. Note that the sail block is not shown.

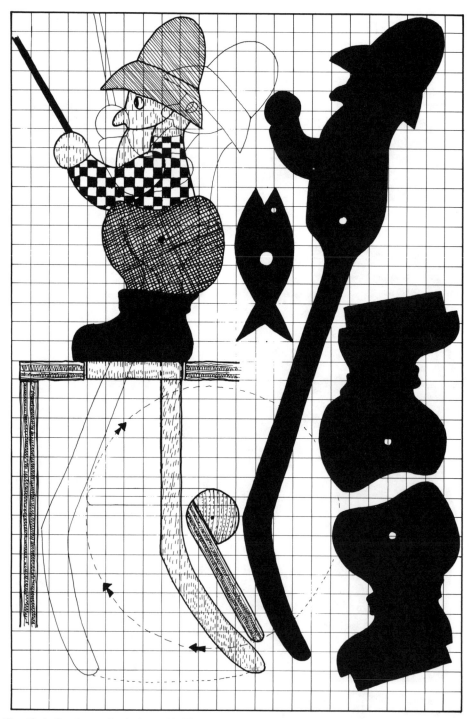

Fig. 13-4. Cutting and painting grid. The scale is about 3 grid squares to 1 inch. Note that the trip lever catches the hooked lever or leg and sets the fisherman in motion. The fish is drilled, in case you need to add a counterbalance weight.

trip lever, the seesaw tilting of the top half of the man, the way the outside curve of the hooked lever is stopped by the side of the box, and the "pull-back" function of the weighted fish.

Study the cross section details which show that the man is made up of three plywood thicknesses: two layers for the trousers and a single layer for the man's torso. The torso is pivoted through the trousers, and the hooked lever runs down between the trouser halves and into the box. This is one of the simpler projects, but does require accurate cutting and fitting. The relationship between the sweep of the trip lever and the curve of the hooked lever is critical.

MAKING A WORKING MODEL

When you have studied all the illustrations and details, draw up your designs to size and make tracings. Pencil press transfer the traced shapes of the trousers and the man through to the sheet of cardboard. Then cut out the two forms and use pins and tape to build a flat working model.

Pass a pin through the trousers and the man, and fix him to a wooden workboard. Then draw out the shape of the box, and cut a piece of card to represent

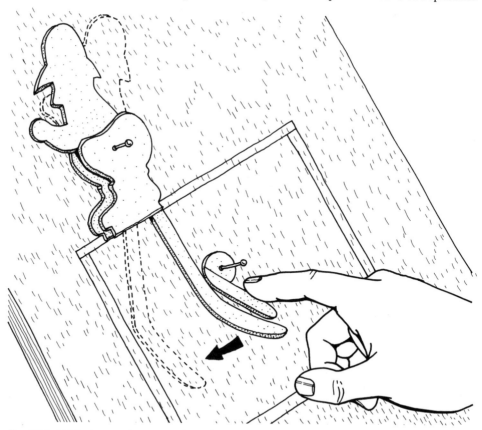

Fig. 13-5. With the moving parts pivoted out on a workboard, turn the trip lever in a clockwise direction.

the main shaft and trip lever. Now have a dry run to fix the precise shape, size, and position of the moving parts. With the two moving parts pivoted on the work-board (FIG. 13-5), slowly turn the trip lever in a clockwise direction until it lifts the hooked extension and tilts the man. If necessary, reshape one or both parts and/or move the pivot points until you achieve a model with a good movement.

CUTTING, BUILDING, AND FITTING

When you have made a good working model and have fixed the size and placing of the various moving parts, reexamine the cutting plan. Using your cardboard cutouts as a template, transfer the profiles and box sides through to the working face of the plywood. Take the straight saw and cut out the six pieces that go to make up the box. Measure, mark, and drill the two 1-inch-diameter, loose-fit main-shaft holes. Now glue and pin the box together—the four sides and the base (FIG. 13-6).

Swiftly rough out the more complex forms that go to make up the man, then set the partially worked shapes in the vise and use the coping saw to carefully fret out the profiles. Hold the saw so that the blade passes through the wood thickness at an angle of 90° to the working face, and cut out the two trouser/boots and the single head/shoulder/trip arm piece. As you work, maneuver both the saw and the wood so the blade is always presented with the line of next cut, and so that you are cutting slightly to the waste side of the drawn lines (FIG. 13-7). When you have cut out the three forms, take a scrap of sandpaper and rub the cutouts

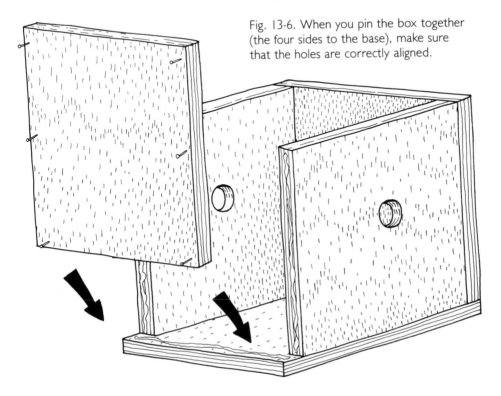

Fig. 13-6. When you pin the box together (the four sides to the base), make sure that the holes are correctly aligned.

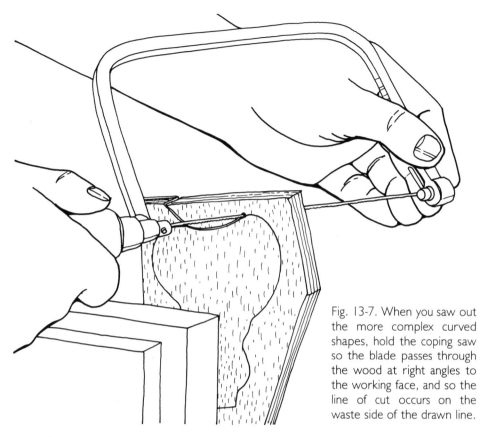

Fig. 13-7. When you saw out the more complex curved shapes, hold the coping saw so the blade passes through the wood at right angles to the working face, and so the line of cut occurs on the waste side of the drawn line.

smooth. Round off the edges of the figure, but leave the boot-to-box tenons and the curved trip arm crisp and square-edged.

Establish the exact size and placing of the man in relation to the sweep of the mainshaft trip lever, then measure and mark out the shape of the tenon/lever mortise hole. Note that, from side to side, the hole has to accommodate the $3/8$-inch-wide tight fit of one boot tenon, the $1/2$-inch-wide loose fit of the curved trip arm, and the other $3/8$-inch-wide tight fit of the other boot tenon. Work a mortise and lever hole with the hand drill, coping saw, and $3/8$-inch chisel.

Allowing for the $1/2$-inch gap between the two boots, slot and glue them side by side in the box lid (FIG. 13-8). Check that they are square and upright, and put the piece to one side until the glue is set.

ASSEMBLING BOX AND FIGURE

When the glue is set, mark in the position of the pivotal split pin holes on the boot/trousers base, and the torso. When the man is carefully lined up and in place, use the drill—with a bit to fit the split pin—to run a loose-fit hole through the three layers of plywood. Remember to place washers at each end of the split pin and between the wood thicknesses, and slide the split pin home. Curl over the ends.

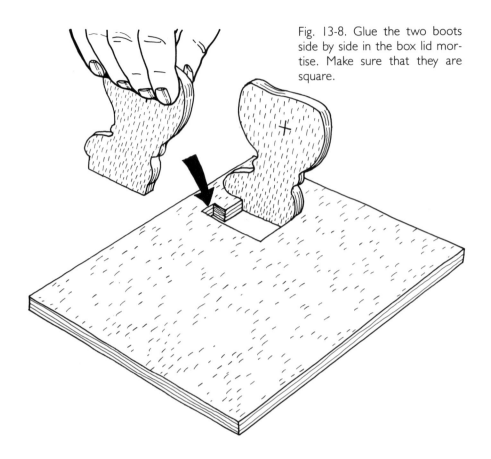

Fig. 13-8. Glue the two boots side by side in the box lid mortise. Make sure that they are square.

Slide the 1-inch diameter mainshaft dowel through the box and mark off the position of the trip lever. Secure the dowel in the vise, and use the coping saw and sandpaper to cut away the small area of dowel waste in order to make a level bed for the 3/8-inch-thick trip lever. Cut, trim, and drill both the lever and the dowel for the final fitting. Now carefully slide the dowel through the box, and glue, fit, and screw the trip lever into position (FIG. 13-9).

Place the lid and figure top on the box and test the movement by turning the mainshaft in a clockwise direction. By sanding the curved arm and sliding the shaft a little to the left or to the right, you can make adjustments until the trip lever and the curved trip arm are perfectly aligned.

Fit, glue, and pin the stop rings on either end of the shaft and screw-fit the lid on the box. Finally, attach the fishing rod and fish (FIG. 13-10).

MAKING THE SAIL AND FITTING THE TAIL VANE

Set the 10-inch long piece of 1-x-2 hardwood out on the workbench. Mark it off sequentially along its length at 3 inches, 2 inches, 2 inches, and 3 inches. Establish the center point and mark off diagonals on the ends. Note that the wood needs to be carefully angled to achieve a sail that turns in a clockwise direction. Use a

Fig. 13-9. Slide the dowel drive shaft through the box and glue and screw the trip lever in position.

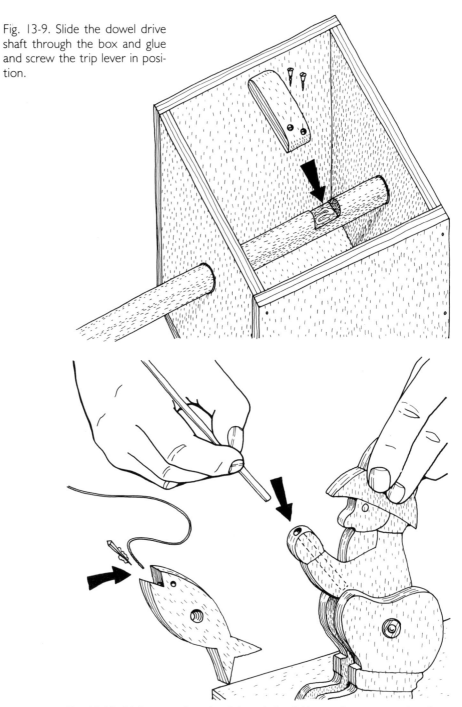

Fig. 13-10. Make sure that the fish and the fishing rod come together for a good fit: drill, glue, and wedge. You might need to add a counterbalance weight to the fish—a nut and bolt, for example.

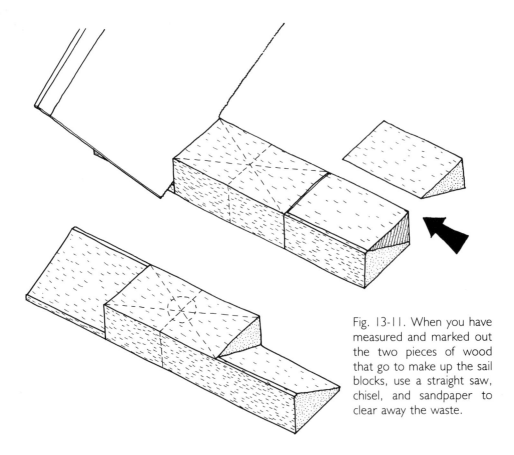

Fig. 13-11. When you have measured and marked out the two pieces of wood that go to make up the sail blocks, use a straight saw, chisel, and sandpaper to clear away the waste.

straight saw, chisel, and sandpaper to cut away the two areas of end waste (FIG. 13-11).

Sand the angled sail block faces until the sail blades can be bedded down to a smooth fit. Use a 1-inch diameter bit and drill the mainshaft hole. Next, glue the angled faces, and butt the sail blades hard up against the sail block stops and secure with brass screws. Slide the sail block on the mainshaft and attach with glue and a screw. Run the screw through the side of the block and into the shaft. Now take the shaped tail vane, which you have rubbed down and finished, and screw it to the side of the drive box. Finally, use a $^1/2$-inch bit and drill two pivotal holes, one in the lid and one in the base (FIG. 13-12).

PAINTING AND FITTING

When the piece is finished, prepare for painting: Clear up all the dust and bench clutter; wipe all surfaces to be painted with a spirit-soaked cloth; and carefully set out all your paints, brushes, and materials. Reexamine the working drawings to decide how the project ought to be painted, and plan out the stages accordingly.

As to your choice of colors: the whale, the man's boots, and the fishing rod could be painted black; the trousers and the waves could be blue; the hat yellow;

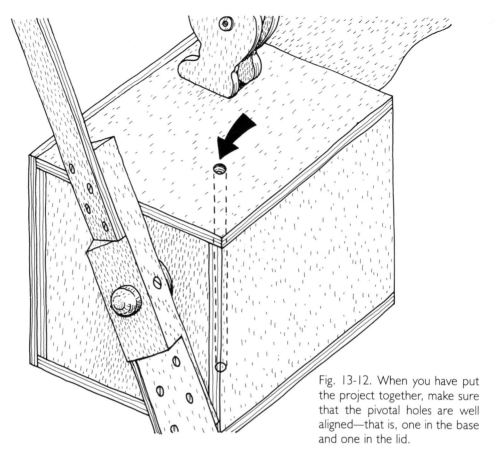

Fig. 13-12. When you have put the project together, make sure that the pivotal holes are well aligned—that is, one in the base and one in the lid.

the shirt red and white, and so on. If you are curious as to how colors will look together, draw a little mock-up on a scrap of wood and have a trial run.

Begin painting by laying on a couple of coats of primer, and work the paint into all the corners and areas that are going to bear the brunt of the weather. Pay particular attention to the top of the box, to joints, and to exposed edges. Follow with an undercoat and then lay on the main blocks of color. Don't forget to let the paint dry out between coats. Lay on the largest areas of color first (the whale, sea, and the sides of the box), and then gradually paint smaller areas and details. Work upwards from the ground colors, all the while picking out details, correcting mistakes, and edging motifs with black lines.

While the paint is drying, bind the top of your chosen post with the galvanized wire and secure the ends with the staples (FIG. 13-13). Now take the drill and 1/2-inch bit, and bore out the top of the post to a depth of about 6 inches. Smear a little grease or oil onto the pivotal rod and drive it down into the top of the post. Ideally about 9 inches of rod should be sticking up from the post. When the post has been well set up in the garden, slide a couple of brass washers on the rod and set the wind machine in place. Finally, give the whole piece a few generous coats of varnish, and the job is done.

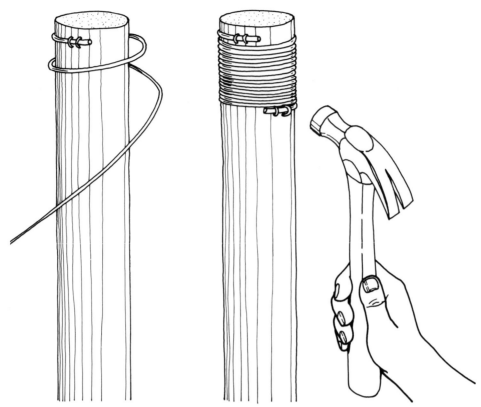

Fig. 13-13. Before you bore out and fit the swing-turn pivot rod hole, strengthen the post by binding the top up with galvanized wire.

HINTS AND MODIFICATIONS

With a project of this character, you do need to work with care and caution; measure twice and cut once. Aim for clean, crisp edges.

The rod and the fish need to be fitted by trial and error.

If, when you come to fitting the box together, you find that the edge-to-edge joints are open or less than perfect, fill with resin filler used on car bodies.

Spookey Indian vibrating windmill

This project draws on many traditions, from American Indian shaman rattles and early pioneer weather vanes, to country-and-western harps and Pennsylvania German music boxes. The vibrating noise sounds Indian, the painted silhouette looks very much like those that were made by pioneer farmers, the twanging music has a country-and-western flavor and the quality of the woodwork appears German-American.

The working action is beautifully simple: The wind turns the shaft, the two cams pluck the metal strips, which vibrate within the box and produce the most beautiful, if slightly eerie, reverberating music. Set this wind machine up in your garden to amuse and delight your family, puzzle your neighbours, and frighten off faint-hearted night prowlers (FIG. 14-1).

TOOLS AND MATERIALS

- [ ] A sheet of 1/4-inch-thick multicore plywood, 24×36 inches
- [ ] A piece of 1 1/2-×-2-inch section wood about 20 inches long, for the propeller
- [ ] A couple of hardwood scraps at about 1×2 inches at 3 inches long, for the two trip cams
- [ ] A 12-inch length of 1-inch-diameter broomstick dowel for the main shaft. Make sure that the wood is free from knots and splits
- [ ] Two hardwood pieces 4−5 inches long: One 1/2×3/4 inches, the other 3/4×3/4 inches. These hold the two metal strips.
- [ ] One hardwood strip 4−5 inches long, for the bridge strip
- [ ] Two 1/2-inch-wide springy steel strips 6−7 inches long, for the vibrating blades. You could use clock springs or packing case strapping
- [ ] A piece of 1/2-inch-diameter steel rod about 14 inches long, for the pivot shaft
- [ ] Resin glue
- [ ] A selection of brass screws and pins/nails about 1/2 inch long
- [ ] A can of blackboard paint for the Indian silhouette
- [ ] A can of yacht varnish   □ A pencil and ruler
- [ ] A compass and try square
- [ ] A large sheet each of graph paper and tracing paper   (Continued)

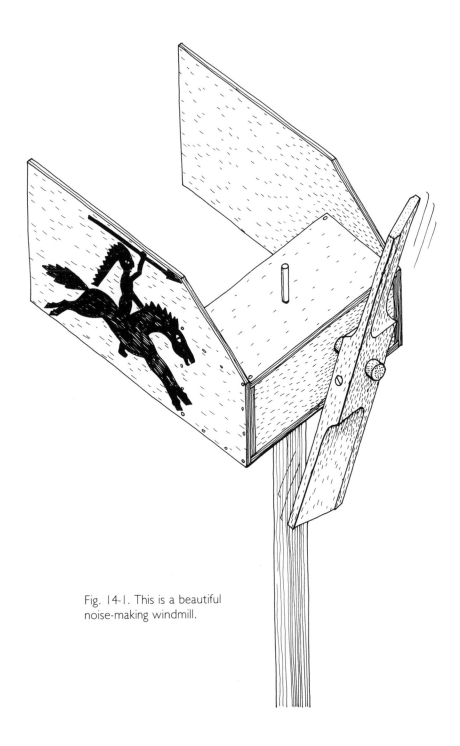

Fig. 14-1. This is a beautiful noise-making windmill.

☐ A workbench   ☐ A straight saw   ☐ A coping saw
☐ A hand drill with ⁵/₈-inch and 1-inch bits
☐ A drawknife   ☐ A holdfast or G-clamp   ☐ A rasp
☐ A pack of graded sandpapers   ☐ A screwdriver
☐ A selection of paint brushes

DESIGN AND TECHNIQUE

Examine the working drawings (FIGS. 14-2, 14-3, and 14-4). The simple two-strip, two-cam mechanism is contained in a small, easy-to-make box. Notice the knife-worked, one-piece propeller, and the two tail vanes—one on each side of the box. It's worth noting that, although assembly is straightforward, you might have some difficulty when fitting the two metal strips. These are held between two glued and screwed strips. Finally, note how the two metal strips run over a small bridge strip. The diagramatic cutting plan in FIG. 14-3 allows for spares, in case the first fitting does not work.

DRAWING AND CUTTING

When you have studied the workings drawings and you have a clear idea as to how the various parts are cut, worked, fitted, and assembled, draw the design up to full size. Check and double check all the measurements, to make sure that you haven't made any mistakes, then trace off the lines of the design and pencil press transfer the traced lines through to the working face of the various pieces of wood. When the lines are clearly established, label all parts and faces. Now you are ready to begin cutting the pieces out.

First use the straight saw to rip the wood down into manageable component parts (FIG. 14-5), then follow with the coping saw to cut out the more complex profiles. Finally, when you have fixed the position of the various shaft holes, use the drill to clear out the waste.

BUILDING THE BOX

With the two long sides and the two ends, have a trial dry fitting. Arrange the sides so that the box corners can be pin-fixed through from the ends. When you have worked out the order of work, align the shaft holes. Then smear a little glue onto the end edges of the long sides, and fit the ends with the pins. After fixing the four sides, turn the box over so that its top edge is down on the worksurface. Carefully glue the uppermost edge (the bottom of the box). Then take the bottom sheet, check the position of the pivot hole, make sure that the box is square, and attach it with glue and pins.

When the glue is set, temporarily screw-fit the box lid (FIG. 14-6). Use the graded sandpapers to rub the wood down to a smooth, ready-to-paint finish. When all the corners and exposed cut edges are nicely rounded, rub the drive shaft hole out with a scrap of sandpaper until the 1-inch-diameter dowel shaft is a loose, easy fit. Finally, unscrew and remove the box lid.

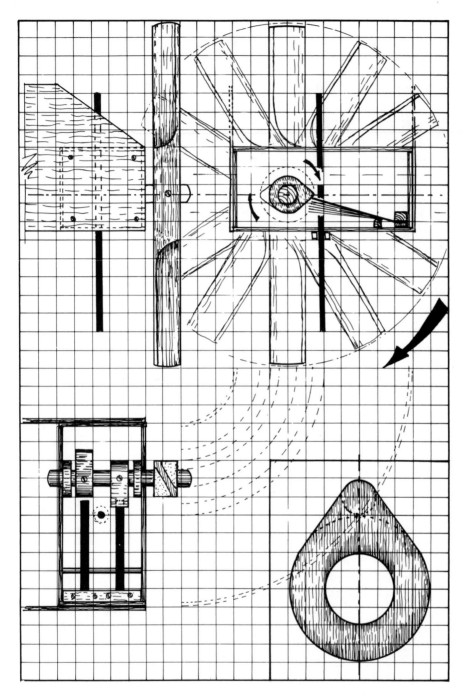

Fig. 14-2. Working drawing. At a scale of 1 grid square to 1 inch, the box measures about 5 × 10 × 4¹/₂ inches. Note that it is important which way the propeller turns; the cams need to press down onto the metal strips (top). Cam detail. The scale is 4 squares to 1 inch (bottom).

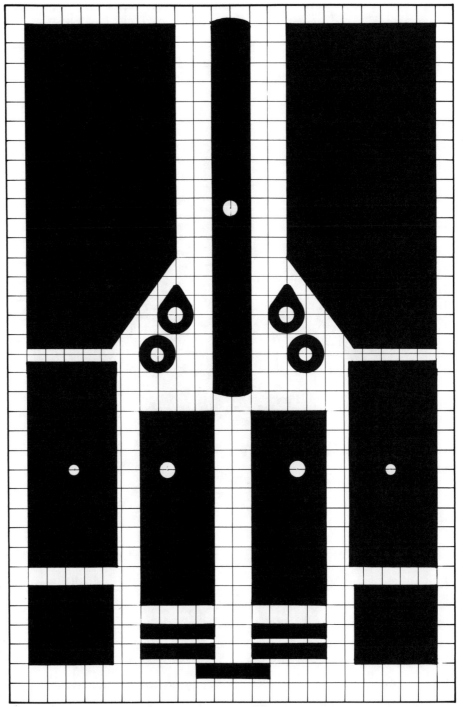

Fig. 14-3. Cutting grid. The scale is 1 grid square to 1 inch (with allowance for spare bridge strips).

Fig. 14-4. Painting grid. The scale is 2 grid squares to 1 inch. Bear in mind that the design needs to be reversed and worked on two tail vane boards.

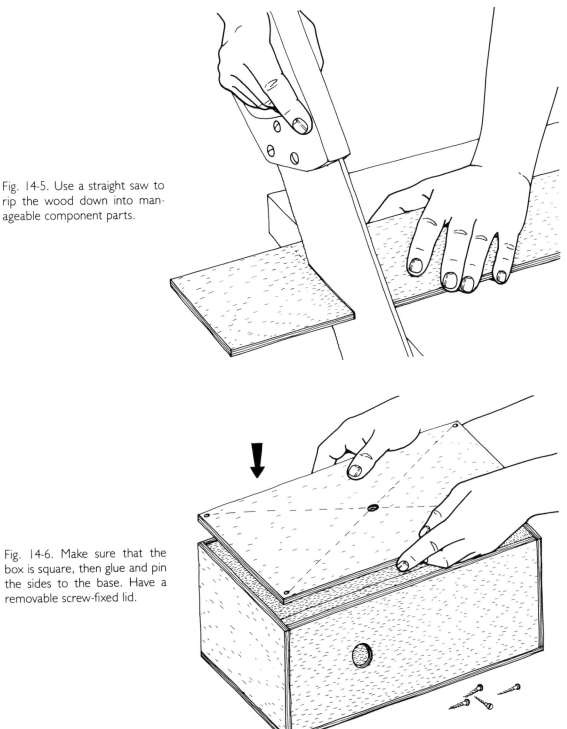

Fig. 14-5. Use a straight saw to rip the wood down into manageable component parts.

Fig. 14-6. Make sure that the box is square, then glue and pin the sides to the base. Have a removable screw-fixed lid.

FITTING THE METAL STRIPS

Set the box right-side up on the worksurface so that the end with the two drive shaft holes is nearest to you—that is, the front of the box facing left and the back of the box facing right. Identify and mark the position of the two metal blades: they should spring out of the end of the box furthest from the drive shaft holes. Now take the $1/2$-x-$3/4$-inch fixing strip, cut it to length, and glue and pin-fix it across the far bottom end of the box. Glue the two metal blades in position on the base strip. If all is correct, the metal blades should be set about $1^1/2$ inches apart—about $1^1/4$ inches away from the box sides and parallel to each other. When you are happy with the position of the two blades, glue and screw the $3/4$-x-$3/4$-inch wood strip on top of the first so that the metal blades are firmly sandwiched and held (FIG. 14-7).

Finally, take the $3/4$-x-$1/2$-inch strip and cut out the bridge shape using the coping saw. Rub the edges down to a smooth round-edged finish, then screw the strip under the metal blades. Aim to have the bridge set about 1 inch away from the sandwich strips so that the blades are cocked up at an angle (FIG. 14-8).

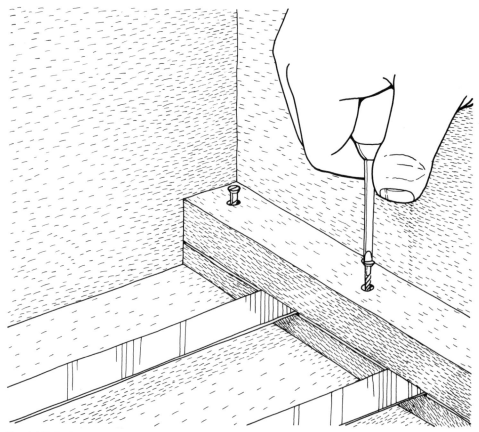

Fig. 14-7. When you come to fitting the two metal strips, sandwich them between two fixings strips—one at $1/2 \times 3/4$ inches and the other at $3/4 \times 3/4$ inches. Use glue and screws.

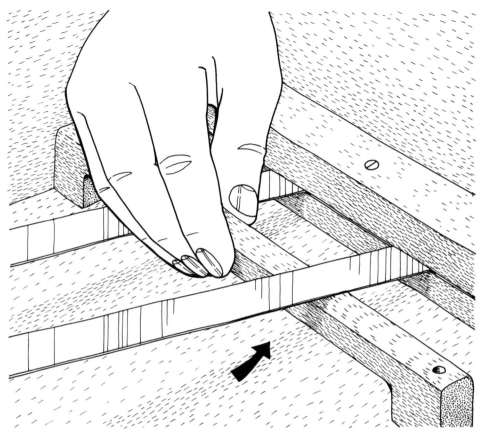

Fig. 14-8. Cut the bridge from the $1/2$-×-$3/4$-inch hardwood strip, slide it under the metal strips, and attach with screws. The metal strips need to be cocked up at a slight angle.

FITTING THE DRIVE SHAFT

Take the 1-inch-diameter dowel, the two stop rings and the two trip cams, and thread the dowel through the box and through the four components. The fitting order of rings and cams on the shaft is: ring, cam, cam, ring. Screw-fix the rings and cams so that the rings are set hard up against the inside of the box, and so that the cams are lined up with the metal strips. Set the cams around the shaft at $0°$ and $180°$—that is, at the 12 o'clock and 6 o'clock positions (FIG. 14-9). If all is correct, in any single complete turn of the shaft, the plucking sequence or timing will be equally spaced out. When you are satisfied with the arrangement, screw down the lid.

MAKING AND FITTING THE PROPELLER

Using a pencil, ruler, and set square, mark the 20-inch length of 2-×-$1^{1}/2$-inch section wood off along its length at $7^{1}/2$ inches, $2^{1}/2$ inches, $2^{1}/2$ inches, and $7^{1}/2$ inches. Establish the center point on the 2-inch-wide front face. Then use the

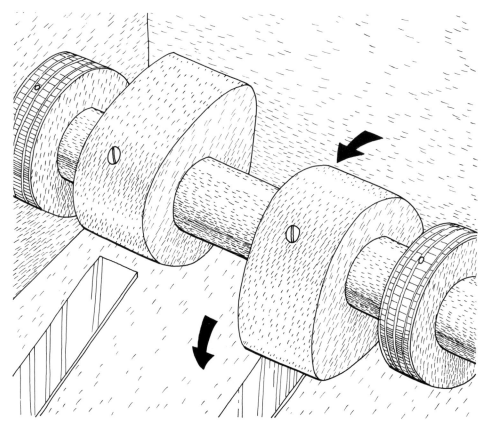

Fig. 14-9. Fix the cams on the drive shaft so that they are set at 0° and 180°—or 12 o'clock and 6 o'clock positions.

drill with the 1-inch bit and —being very careful that the drill passes through the wood at 90° to the front face—bore out the propshaft hole. Set the wood front-face up on the worksurface and, one end at a time, pencil in diagonals that go from bottom left, to top right. Aiming for a propeller blade thickness of about $1/4$ inch. Shade in all the areas that need to be cut away (FIG. 14-10).

With the wood clamped securely to the bench, take the drawknife and slice out the large areas of waste. Work from center to end, all the while drawing the knife along the length of the wood. Don't try to remove the wood in large chops, but in small slices and slivers (FIG. 14-11). Continue working the wood from face to face and end to end, until you have achieved the propeller form.

Finally, when you have rubbed the wood down to a smooth finish, and rounded off the edges and ends, slide the propeller on the drive shaft and fix with a brass screw.

DECORATING THE TAIL VANES AND FINISHING

Set the two tail vanes out symmetrically on the workbench. Label the front face of each vane, identifying the face that needs to be decorated. From vane to vane,

Fig. 14-10. Making and fitting the propeller. Mark off along the wood at $7^1/2$ inches, $2^1/2$ inches, $2^1/2$ inches and $7^1/2$ inches (top). Establish the center point and drill a 1-inch-diameter drive shaft hole. Draw out all the lines that go to make up the design and shade in the areas that need to be cut away (middle). Slice away the waste to achieve the characteristic propeller shape (bottom).

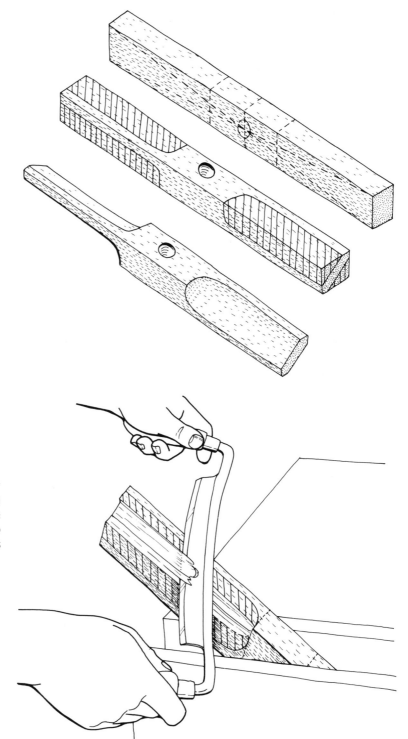

Fig. 14-11. Clamp the propeller to the bench and use the drawknife to clear away the waste. Work from center to end, drawing the knife towards you.

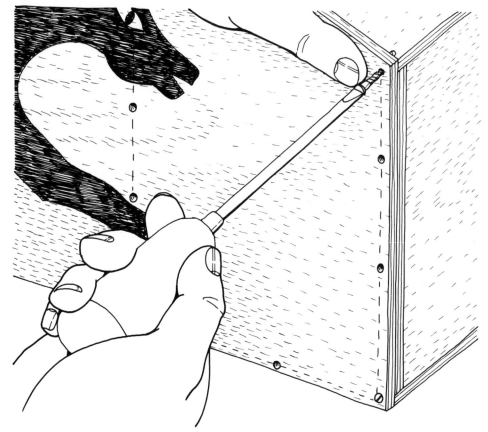

Fig. 14-12. Finally, screw the two tail vanes: one on either side of the box.

reverse the tracing paper so that the image always looks to front. Trace off your chosen image and pencil press transfer the traced lines through to the front face.

Note: A traditional nineteenth century design was used here, but you can modify it to suit your own needs.

When you have a crisp, bold outline, use the matte black paint and block in the image. Don't fiddle around with fussy details, but try for a strong, clean dynamic silhouette—an image that can be read from a distance.

When the paint is dry, screw the vanes to either side of the box (FIG. 14-12). Then bore a $1/2$-inch diameter hole down into the top of the display post, sink the pivot rod down into the hole, drop a washer on the rod, and slide the wind machine into position.

With the machine turned and carefully tied back so that the propeller is out of the wind, take a broad brush and lay on several coats of clear yacht varnish. Finally, cut the string ties and stand well back—and watch, listen, and enjoy!

HINTS AND MODIFICATIONS

Although this machine only has two vibrating strips, there's no reason why you can't modify the design and have more.

If you want to vary the pitch of the sounds, consider using: metal strips of a different width and length, larger or smaller cams, or even strips of bamboo.

If you do decide to build a large machine—one with many sounding strips—then you will have to either increase the length and width of the propeller, or modify the design and use a four-bladed X-type propeller.

15

American Indian in a canoe whirligig

In times past, just about every town, village, and farm in America boasted one or more weather vanes. They didn't have to be fancy—just good, strong metal or wood images set high up on masts and roof tops. Horses, roosters, angels, mermaids, fish, soldiers, and trains were all very common weather vane subjects. However, perhaps the most popular designs of all, and certainly the most useful, were the Red Indians. They were useful, because in pioneer days, not only did the vane swing in the wind and warn of bad weather, but the Indian images let bands of raiding Indians know that the land had been fairly traded (FIG. 15-1).

TOOLS AND MATERIALS

- ☐ A piece of 1-inch-thick multicore plywood, 12×6 inches
- ☐ A piece of straight-grained 1-×-$^1/_2$-inch sectioned wood about 12 inches long, for the propeller
- ☐ A short length of $^1/_4$-inch-diameter hardwood dowel for the body/arms pivot rod
- ☐ A 6-inch length of coathanger wire for the base pivot shaft
- ☐ Three brass washers: two to fit the hardwood dowel and one to fit the coathanger wire
- ☐ Resin glue   ☐ Acrylic paints, colors to suit
- ☐ A can of yacht varnish
- ☐ A pencil and ruler   ☐ A sheet each of graph paper and tracing paper
- ☐ A workbench with a vise   ☐ A coping saw or scroll saw
- ☐ A hand drill with a good selection of bits   ☐ A rasp
- ☐ A selection of stick tools that can be wrapped around sandpaper when sanding difficult shapes
- ☐ A pack of graded sandpapers   ☐ A selection of brushes

DESIGN AND TECHNIQUE

Examine the working drawings details (FIGS. 15-2 and 15-3) and note how the simple design makes for an easy-to-work project. The pivot is a loose fit in the body and a tight fit in the arms/propellers. The two half-prop arms are easily worked and whittled from a single length of wood. When you have noted all the details

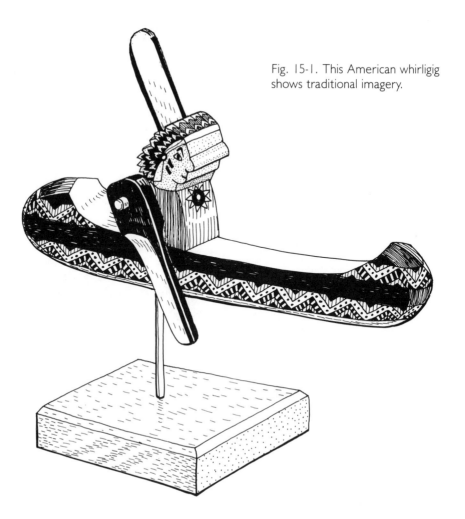

Fig. 15-1. This American whirligig shows traditional imagery.

and features that go to make up the design, use a pencil and ruler to draw the design to full size (FIG. 15-3). The canoe should be about 12 inches long.

When choosing wood for the prop-arms, make sure that it is straight-grained, easy to work, and free from splits, stains and knots.

TRANSFERRING, CUTTING, AND ROUNDING

When you have achieved a crisp, workable design, trace off the profile and pencil press transfer the traced lines through to the working face of the 1-inch plywood (FIG. 15-4). Make sure that the profile is well defined. Carefully mark in the position of the arm pivot, then use the hand drill and the 3/8-inch bit to bore out the waste. With the wood well secured, either in the jaws of a vise or with clamps, use the coping saw and—with the blade passing through the wood at 90° to the working face—cut out the form. If you are using a scroll saw, hold the wood and guide it firmly with both hands. Make sure that the line of cut is on the waste side of the drawn line (FIG. 15-5).

American Indian in a canoe whirligig   179

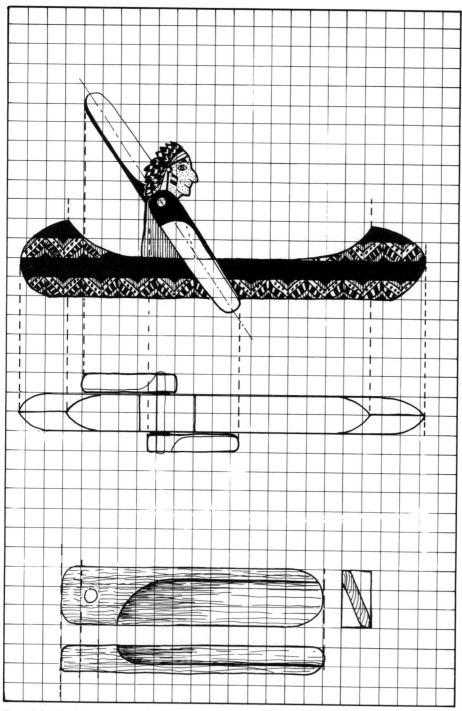

Fig. 15-2. Working drawing. At a grid scale of 2 grid squares to 1 inch, the canoe measures about 11 – 12 inches long.

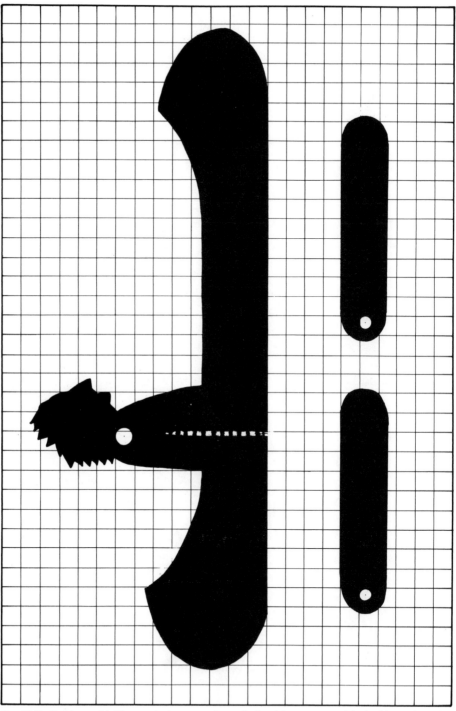

Fig. 15-3. Cutting grid. The scale is approximately 3 grid squares to 1 inch. Note that the propeller arms need to be cut from an easy-to-work hardwood.

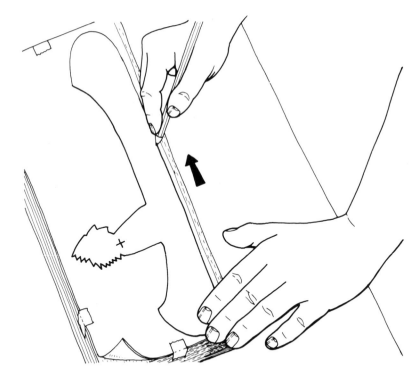

Fig. 15-4. Trace off the profile, and pencil press transfer the traced lines through to the working face of the 1-inch-thick plywood.

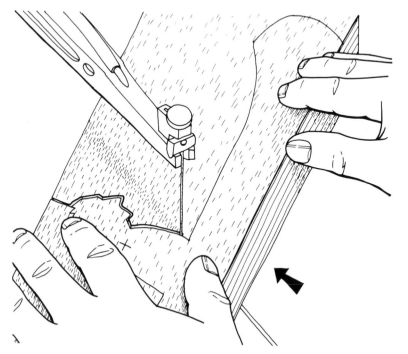

Fig. 15-5. When you are working with a scroll saw, hold the wood firmly and guide it with both hands. Make sure that the line of cut is a little on the waste side of the drawn lines.

When you have cut out the Indian canoe shape, reexamine (FIG. 15-2) and note how the canoe shape is slightly rounded at both ends and at the base. Draw a center line and establish the areas that need to be worked. With the wood secured flat-face down on the worksurface, use the rasp and work from the top flat-face down to edge center (FIG. 15-6). Run the tool from the flat side face of the canoe and around the cut edges until you achieve the boat shape. Then use the graded sandpapers, work the profile to a smooth finish. Use sandpaper wrapped around a stick to bring out the crisp, modeled forms at the nose, chin, and feathered head dress. If the wood crumbles, you might need to patch it with a resin filler.

Finally, set the canoe in the vise with the bottom edge up and bore out the swing/display pivot hole (FIG. 15-7). Refer to the cutting plan in FIG. 15-3 for the position of the holes.

WHITTLING THE PROPELLER

Divide the 12-inch length of 1-×½-inch propeller wood in half lengthwise. Mark in the position of the two ¼-inch-diameter pivot holes, then drill them out. Mark off each end with a single diagonal—that is, with a corner-to-corner line that runs from bottom left corner to top right. One face at a time, set the wood flat down on the worksurface and mark in all the straight and curved lines that go to make up the design. Shade in the resultant forms so that you know exactly which areas

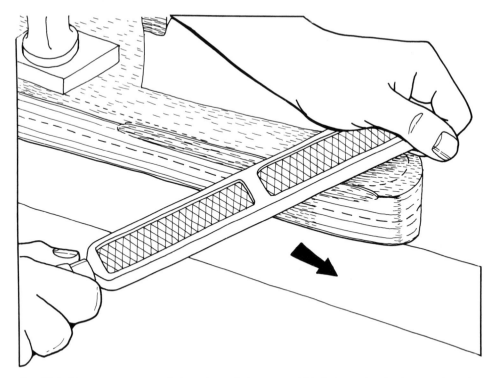

Fig. 15-6. Use a rasp to round the edges of the canoe. Work from the flat face to the edge center.

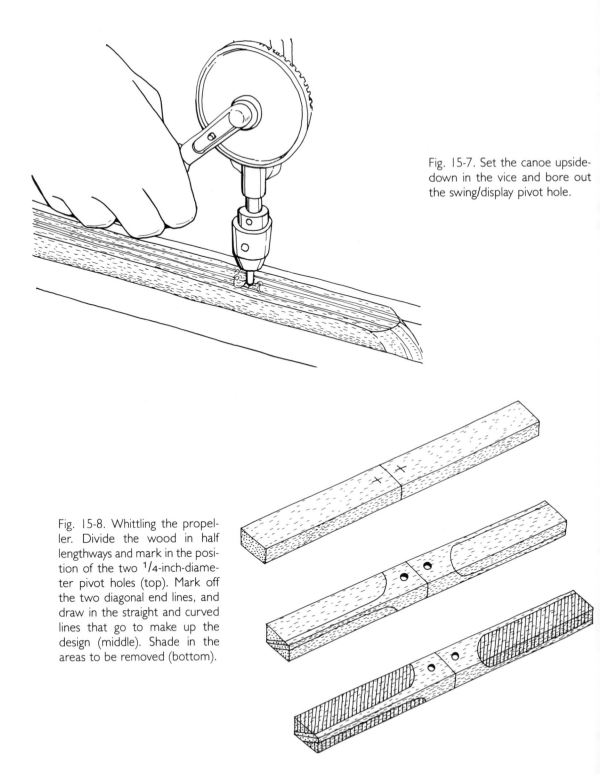

Fig. 15-7. Set the canoe upside-down in the vice and bore out the swing/display pivot hole.

Fig. 15-8. Whittling the propeller. Divide the wood in half lengthways and mark in the position of the two $1/4$-inch-diameter pivot holes (top). Mark off the two diagonal end lines, and draw in the straight and curved lines that go to make up the design (middle). Shade in the areas to be removed (bottom).

need to be removed (FIG. 15-8). If you have any doubts as to how the wood is shaped, take a scrap of soft wood and make a working model. Note that, from end to end, the face of the propeller characteristically angles and twists.

When you are clear as to which part of the wood needs to be cut away, take the wood in one hand and the knife in the other, and slice away the waste little by little (FIG. 15-9). One side at a time, work the length of wood from center to end, slicing and paring away the waste until you are left with the prop form. Finally, use the coping saw to round off the ends and edges, then saw through the center so that you have the two identical half-prop arms. Rub the wood down to a smooth finish that is ready for painting.

PAINTING

Before you begin, keep in mind that paint layers add to the total thickness and therefore reduce hole sizes. Take a scrap of sandpaper and rub out the through-body hole so that it is a very loose fit. Then, wipe the wood over with a slightly damp cloth. Decide how you are going to support the work while it is being painted: Are you going to hang it on cotton threads or support it on a wire rack?

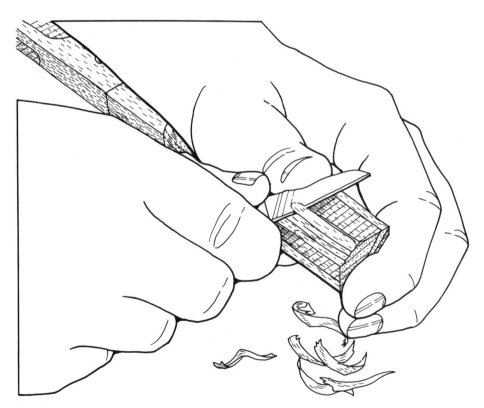

Fig. 15-9. Take the wood in one hand and the knife in the other and slice away the waste with little thumb-supported paring cuts.

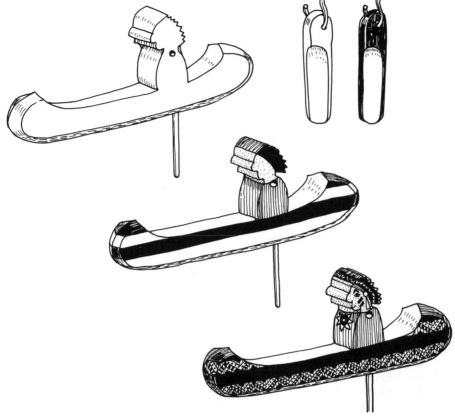

Fig. 15-10. Painting. Lay on the white undercoat (top). Lay on the main areas of colored ground (middle). Pick out all the patterns and details with a fine-point brush (bottom).

Re-examine the painting grid (FIG. 15-2). Then, lay on a white undercoat, the top coat, and all the decorative details that go to make up the design (FIG. 15-10). Don't ladle the paint on in great daubs, but rather in thin, carefully brushed coats. Finally, use a knife to pare out the various pivot holes, then lay on a few coats of clear varnish.

ASSEMBLY

When the varnish is completely dry, pass the hardwood dowel through the loose-fit body hole, and slide the washers on the dowel. Dab the ends of the dowel with a little resin glue and then fit the two prop-arms. Set the arms one up and one down so that they follow through on the same axis (FIG. 15-11). When the glue is dry, trim the dowel ends back to just above the surface and dab them with varnish. Finally, push the wire pivot into the base hole. Set the finished whirligig out on a post in the garden, or indoors on an exhibition plinth block.

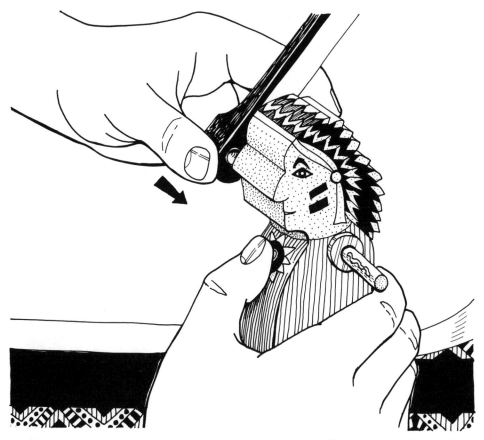

Fig. 15-11. Pass the dowel through the loose-fit body hole, slide on the washers, dab the ends of the dowel with resin glue, and attach the two propeller arms—one up and one down.

HINTS AND MODIFICATIONS

This particular flatwood design is very basic; if you want to build a more complex form, sandwich several layers of wood.

You could use a nut and bolt pivot rather than the hardwood dowel. If you do, use brass or stainless steel.

If you decide to use enamel paints rather than water-based acrylics, allow extra time for drying.

Glossary

Acrylic Paint   A plastic PVA-type paint. Acrylics are perfect for whirligig making: They can be used straight from the tube, the colors are bright, and they dry so fast that several coats can be applied in the space of an hour. Because whirligigs and wind machines are exposed to the weather, it's best to protect the painted surfaces with yacht varnish.

Automaton   In the context of this book, a wind-driven machine, robot, or device that appears to run under its own hidden power. Many of these whirligigs and wind machines draw their inspiration from traditional nineteenth century English and American models that, in turn, were modeled after older German and Swiss music boxes, clocks, and toys.

Beam Compass   A compass used to draw large arcs and circles that are too big to be drawn with a two-leg compass. You can make your own beam compass from a piece of straight wood: Drill a hole for a pencil at one end and a selection of pivot holes at the other. The required radius is fixed by moving a screw or nail pivot point backwards or forwards along the line of holes (FIG. G-1).

Bearing   In the context of this book, a support, guide, or locating piece for a turning shaft or pivot. Ideally, bearings turn smoothly and easily, and to this end wood-to-wood bearings need to be waxed and metal-to-metal bearings greased or oiled.

Beech   A heavy, pleasant, reddish brown hardwood that is good for turning, and useful for making wind machine movements such as trip levers, cams, shafts, and sail blocks.

Blank   A prepared, ready-to-work block or slab of wood.

Bow Saw   A saw with an H-shaped wooden frame and a slender, flexible blade. It is used for cutting thin section wood.

Box   In the context of this book, the enclosed body or container that houses and protects all the moving parts.

Broomstick Dowel   A round wooden dowel or rod, usually measuring between $3/4 - 1^1/4$ inches in diameter.

Bush or Bushing   A thin metal tube or sleeve serving as a guide or lining for a bearing or shaft.

Calipers   A two-legged measuring instrument used for checking sizes and stepping off set measurments. The best types are those with screw adjustments.

Cam   A rotating offset disc or lever attached to a drive shaft. As the cam turns, it sets in motion other parts of the machine (FIG. G-2).

Centers   In a woodturning, the pivotal points at either end of the lathe. In basic "prong chuck" or "between center" turning, the wood is held, pivoted, and worked between the two center points.

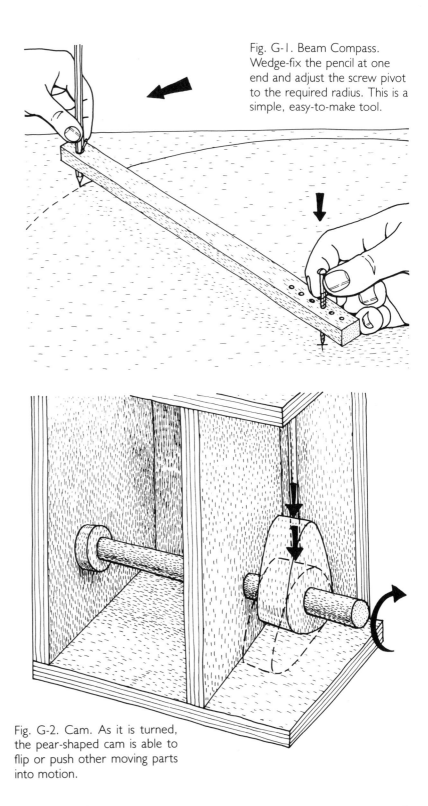

Fig. G-1. Beam Compass. Wedge-fix the pencil at one end and adjust the screw pivot to the required radius. This is a simple, easy-to-make tool.

Fig. G-2. Cam. As it is turned, the pear-shaped cam is able to flip or push other moving parts into motion.

Centering The act of mounting the wood on the lathe and roughing out the initial cylinder. Starting with square section wood, the ends are first of all marked off with diagonals and inscribed with circles; tangents are marked to the circles to produce octagons; and the waste wood is identified and removed with a drawknife, plane, or rasp. Next, the almost round section of wood is pushed or tapped onto the pronged drive center, the tailstock is brought up towards the work and clamped into position. The dead center is wound up and driven into the wood, and the tool rest is fixed so that it is just clear of the work. Finally, the tool grasped with in both hands and steadied on the tool rest and the initial cylinder is roughed out.

Clamps, Cramps, or Holdfasts Screw devices used for holding wood while it is being worked or accurately cut. These are also called G-clamps, C-clamps, and strap clamps.

Close-Grained Wood that appears to have evenly set annual rings. This is usually good wood for working.

Compass A two-legged instrument used for drawing circles and arcs.

Coping Saw A small, fine-bladed frame saw used for cutting out thin section wood and board. This is the perfect saw for cutting out holes and for working enclosed corners and curves; the blade can be quickly removed and refitted (FIG. G-3).

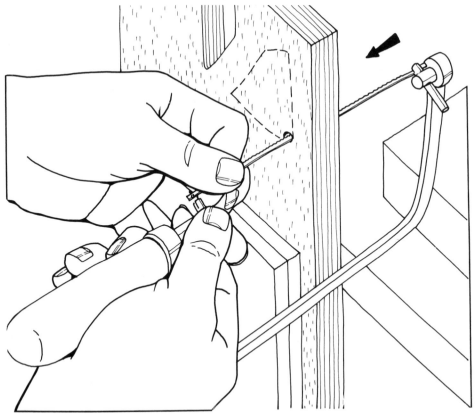

Fig. G-3. Coping Saw. When cutting out an enclosed hole, remove the blade, pass one end through the pilot hole, fit the blade back into the frame, and adjust the tension.

Counterbalance Many wind machines use a counterbalance for the motive force—usually it's a seesaw-like weight or extension that balances or offsets another.

Craft Knife A knife with a short, sharp, easy-to-change blade.

Cut-In In woodturning, the act of sliding the parting tool or the skew chisel directly into the wood. Or, a general woodworking term used to describe the act of making an initial cut.

Cutouts The plywood shapes that go to make up the project, also called profiles or silhouettes.

Designing The process of working out shapes, structures, forms, functions, and details. For these projects, museum originals were drawn and measured with the details modified to suit. Then working models were made using found bits of thin wood, card, and string. Further modifications and adjustments were made, and the final full size measured designs drawn-up.

Dome-Head Tacks Small brass, round-headed tacks, pins, or nails are used in upholstery.

Drawknife A traditional two handled knife used for cutting and carving free forms. In use, the workpiece is supported in a clamp or vise, and the tool drawn along the work towards the user.

Drilling For these projects an easy-to-use, hand-operated breast drill is best. Such a drill accepts large and small bit sizes, can drill holes at speed, is inexpensive, and is totally controllable. In use, the work is backed with a piece of scrap and held firm with clamps (FIG. G-4).

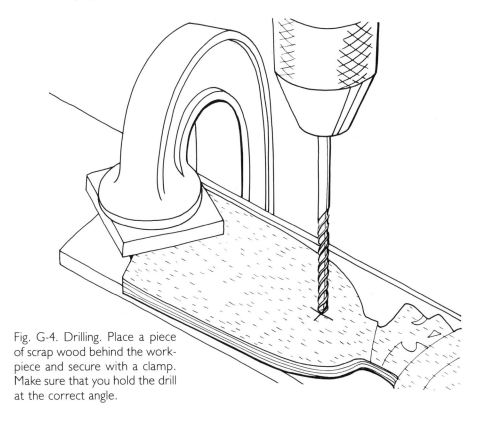

Fig. G-4. Drilling. Place a piece of scrap wood behind the workpiece and secure with a clamp. Make sure that you hold the drill at the correct angle.

Drive Shaft   The main shaft that links the propeller/sails to the moving parts.

Enamel Paints   Gloss-finish, oil-based paints suitable for exterior use.

Files   Tools used to shape wood. Files come in all shapes and sizes.

Fillers   Material used to fill breaks, cavities, and scratches in wood. It is good for filling the cut edges of multi core plywood prior to finishing and painting. Use a stable two tube plastic/resin autobody filler, one that can be sanded, sawn and drilled.

Finial   In the context of this book, an ornamental topping. Found items such as wooden balls, plastic castings, beads, and small decorative turnings work well for these projects.

Finishing   The process of filling, sanding, rubbing down, staining, painting, varnishing, and otherwise bringing the work to a satisfactory structural, textural, mechanical, and visual conclusion.

Galvanized Rod   Mild steel rod that has been given a protective coat of zinc. Heavy grade fencing wire and coathanger wire are both very useful in these projects.

Graph Paper   Paper on which all the pre-project notes, details, and sketches are worked out. For these projects, hardcover sketch books were used for all the initial designs and the small details, and huge lengths of end-of-roll printer's paper for the full-size patterns.

Gridded Working Drawing   A drawing or set of plans that has been drawn to a scaled grid size. If, for example, the scale of the grid is described as "four grid squares to 1 inch," each one of the grid squares can be read off as a $1/4$-inch unit of measurement. If you want to change the scale, draw up a larger grid and transfer the image one square at a time (FIG. G-5).

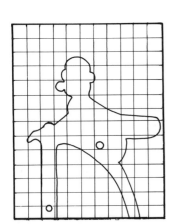
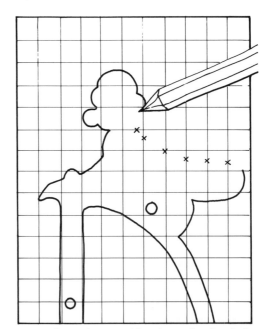

Fig. G-5. Grids. To change the scale, draw up a smaller or larger grid and transfer the design one square at a time.

Hardwood Wood from a deciduous tree. Woods that are straight-grained weather-resistant, and free from knots and splits are best for these projects. Good types are lime, parana pine, holly, fruit tree woods, and cedar.

Headstock In wood turning, the power-driven unit at the left end of the lathe. The headstock carries two trust bearings in which the spindle or mandrel revolves. The power is supplied to the spindle by an electric motor and a drive belt. The spindle has an external screw for chucks and faceplates, and an internal taper for the pronged center.

Lathe A woodworking machine for cutting round sections. The wood is pivoted between centers and spun against a handheld cutting tool. (Note: For lathe safety:

☐ Make sure that faceplate work is well mounted and secure
☐ Turn the work over by hand and make sure that it is clear of the tool rest
☐ Tie back your hair, roll up your sleeves, and make sure that children and pets are out of harm's way
☐ Stop the motor before testing with a template or with callipers
☐ Move the rest well out of the way before sanding
☐ Wear safety glasses
☐ Make sure that your chosen wood is non-toxic
☐ Hold all the tools firmly
☐ Make sure that the switch is within easy reach—never reach over the lathe while it is running.

Leading Edge The forward edge of a propeller or sail blade—the edge that points into the wind and looks in the direction of spin (FIG. G-6).

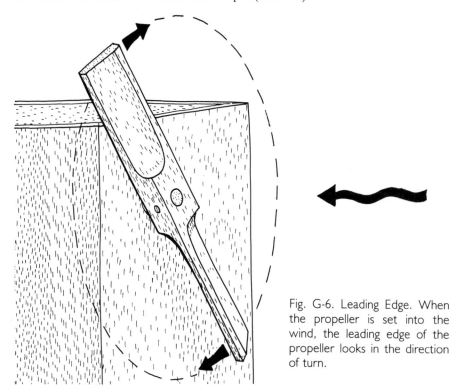

Fig. G-6. Leading Edge. When the propeller is set into the wind, the leading edge of the propeller looks in the direction of turn.

Lever A bar or seesaw-type rod used to lift or set another part into motion.

Lock Washer A special tabbed safety washer that is clenched between the nut and the work or between two nuts. The tabs are bent down over the nut to prevent it from coming loose.

Mating Faces Surfaces that touch.

Maquette A small working model or prototype. If, after drawing up the design, you are unsure how one part might work or fit in relation to another, then you need to make a maquette from card, plastercine, modeling clay or cheap wood.

Masking Tape A sticky contact adhesive tape useful in the workshop. Use it for masking off areas when you are painting, for holding down working drawings, or for strapping up work that has been glued, for example.

Mast In the context of this book, a post, pole, staff, beam, or roof finial on which a whirligig or wind machine is mounted. In all instances it is important that the pivotal fixing—the swivel fixing between the post and the machine—is safe, sound, and smooth running. If you do decide to set a post in the ground, dig it well in, support its base with concrete, and make sure that the top of the post is above head height.

Master Design The final measured working drawing, from which all other details are taken.

Movement The drive mechanism: all the turning, spinning, rolling, swinging and otherwise moving levers, cams, washers, springs and strings that go to make up the project (FIG. G-7).

Multicore or Multiply Laminated plywood used for making whirligigs and wind machines. Always use a close-grained, exterior-grade plywood. Marine grade works well: it is waterproof and has two perfect sides or faces. Such a plywood comes in thicknesses ranging from $1/8$ inch through 1 inch. Multi-core ply can easily be cut and all faces and edges worked to a smooth, even finish. Note: if you use a cheap grade furniture ply, the glue might break down and the layers come apart.

Off-Cuts Bits and pieces of scrap wood left over from other projects. These can be saved for small jobs and for making prototypes. Many wood suppliers sell useful off-cuts.

Paddle Blades Solid sails or propeller made up from one or more parts that are fitted to a central hub or block. These sails resemble canoe paddles.

Painting When painting, make sure that the area is clean, dry, and free from dust. Painting is best done in an area apart from the main wood workshop. Set out all your paints and materials, and consider how the objects are going to be supported while they are wet. Depending on size, they might be hung on a line, placed on a wire rack, hung from wire hooks, etc. Ideally, whirligigs and wind machines need to be primed, undercoated, top coated, decorated, and varnished.

Most of the projects are best painted with acrylics only because they are so easy to use: they dry very quickly, several coats of paint can be applied in a short time, the brushes can be washed in water, and the colors are bright. Oil bound paints are also bright and they come in a huge range of wonderful colors, but they take days to dry and all the equipment needs to be cleaned with solvents. If you are a beginner, start with acrylics, then experiment with other paints as you go along.

Pendulum A weight or bob hung on a cord, that swings freely and triggers off some part of the whirligig mechanism. The longer the cord, the slower the swing. Pendulum bobs can be made out of found objects like balls, beads, and stones.

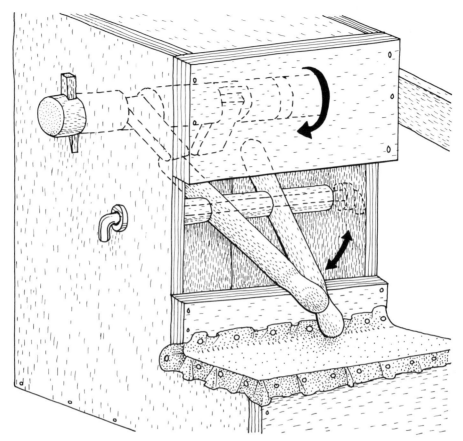

Fig. G-7. Movement refers to all the moving parts.

Pencil Press Transfer Process of transferring the design to the wood. Use a soft 2B pencil for designing and tracing, and a hard H pencil for transferring. The order of work is: Draw out the full size master design, take a careful tracing, pencil in the back of the tracing with a 2B pencil, turn the tracing right side-up and fix it to working surface of the wood with tabs of sticky tape, and finally rework the traced lines with a hard pencil.

Pilot Hole A small guide hole as might be drilled for a larger nail or screw.

Pivot In the context of this book, the point, rod, bolt, rivet, shaft, or dowel on which another part swings, turns, or rolls.

Profiles Any cutout, silhouette, cross-section, or drawn shape.

Propeller or Prop A sail or sail blade that has been cut from one piece of wood. (The drive shaft is often referred to as the prop shaft.)

Prototype A small working model made before starting the project. If you would like to know how the project is going to look, or if you plan modifications, it's best to first make a prototype. Also called a mock-up, dummy, or maquette.

Resin Glue A two-tube adhesive perfect for objects that are going to be exposed to the weather.

Rough Out To chop or cut away the initial waste.

Rub Down To work the sawn profiles and sections to a smooth, ready-to-paint finish. Work well away from the painting area. Trim off the corners, edges, and burrs with a knife or rasp, swiftly rub over with a coarse sandpaper, fill any cracks or holes with car body filler, and finally work through the pack of coarse to smooth graded sandpapers.

Rudder Tail The tail end of the wind machine. If you want the sail to face into the wind and the propeller to spin in one direction, give the machine a long rudder (or vane). The longer the tail rudder or vane, the more likely the machine will always swing around to meet the wind face on.

Scroll Saw A power-driven table or bench saw with a fine blade. The fast up-and-down of the blade results in a swift, fine cut.

Setting In Transferring the working drawings through to the face of the wood and making initial cuts.

Tracing Paper A strong see-through paper used for transferring the lines of the design from the master drawing to the wood.

Trip Lever A bar, rod, dowel, or strip of wood or metal attached to the drive shaft that, in turning, catches, lifts, or pushes down on another part to set that part in motion. (See also Cam)

Try Square Also called a set square or simply a square. Use a square when checking the work for straightness or for 90° angles.

Turning The process of working a round section on a lathe.

Undercoat A flat or non-shiny coat of paint that is applied after the primer and before the top coat. For a good finish, the work needs to be primed, have two undercoats, and a topcoat.

Vane A flat surface designed to catch the wind. The sail, tail, or any one of the flat blades can be considered a vane.

Veer To swing round into the wind and meet it head or face on.

Vice or Vise A bench-mounted screw clamp, used for holding and securing wood while it is being worked.

Workbench This can be anything from a table out in the garage, to an old kitchen table in a spare room, or a special woodworkers bench. The work surface should be the correct height for you, and be firm, strong, and fitted with a vise.

Working Drawings All the sketches, designs, and notes that make up a scaled, measured, full-size drawing.

Working Face The best side of the wood, the side that will show.

Index

A

automobile, crank-starting, windmill, 86

B

bell windmill, 52
bells, 56
bicycle, penny-farthing, clown on,
64
blades, 47-49, 57, 92, 102, 136

C

cams, 174
canoe whirligig, 178
carousel windmill, 139
carving, 19-20, 32-33
center block, 7, 8
chisels, 44
clown on bike windmill, 64
coping saw, 5, 8, 159
crank-starting automobile windmill, 86
cylinders, turning on lathe, 27, 31,
32, 109-111

D

dovecote windmill, 115
drawknife, 175
drilling, 6, 35, 83, 95, 112, 122,
132, 184
drive shafts, 56, 108, 133, 161,
173
drum-beating windmill, 39
Dutch windmill weathervane, 75

F

fisherman windmill, 152

G

gouge, 20

H

hacksaw, 22
Hardy, Thomas, 25
hex designs, 52-54, 60, 61

I

Indian whirligig, 178
Indian windmill, 165

K

Karolik Collection, Boston
Museum of Fine Arts, 25

L

lathe turning, 27, 31, 32, 109-111
leading edges, 124
letter cutting, 82

M

macquettes, 14, 18
mad manikins pop-up windmill,
101
main bearings, 142
mallet, 20
man starting automobile windmill,
86
merry-go-round windmill, 139
models, 14, 18, 157
mounting posts, 23, 49
greasing, 113
nuts, washers in, 84
reinforcing with wire, 164

N

New England soldier whirligig, 1
noise-making windmill, 165

P

paddle-arm Quaker whirligig, 12
pecking bird whirligig, 127
pedal crank, 70, 71
Pennsylvania Dutch hex designs,
52-54, 60, 61
pivot points, 72-73, 122, 157
planing, 81
pop-up figures windmill, 101
projects
American Indian in canoe whirligig, 178
clown on a bike windmill, 64
drum-beating windmill, 39

Dutch windmill weathervane,
75
fisherman windmill, 152
mad manikins pop-up windmill,
101
man starting automobile windmill, 86
merry-go-round windmill, 139
New England soldier whirligig, 1
paddle-arm Quaker whirligig, 12
pecking bird whirligig, 127
spooky Indian vibrating windmill, 165
tinkle-turn dovecote windmill,
115
tubular bell windmill, 52
Yankee Army signalman whirligig, 25
propellers, 136-138, 163, 173,
175, 183, 184, 185
punching holes, 125

Q

Quaker whirligig, paddle-arm, 12

R

rasp, 183
ripping, 171
roughing out, 14, 18
rounding edges, 183

S

sails and sail blocks, 47-49, 57, 92,
102, 136, 142, 160
sanding and finishing, 92, 132
scroll saw, 69, 80, 182
signalman whirligig, Yankee Army,
25
slot cutting, 8, 22
soldier whirligig, New England, 1
spooky Indian vibrating windmill,
165

T

tenon saw, 8
tinkle-turn dovecote windmill, 115
transfers, 179

trip levers, 44, 108
Trumpet Major, The, 25
tubular bell windmill, 52
turning on lathe, 27, 31, 32, 109-111

V

vanes, 142, 160, 174, 176
vibrating windmill, 165

W

weathervanes, Dutch windmill, 75

whirligig
    American development of, vi-vii
    American Indian in canoe, 178
    history of, iv-vi
    New England soldier, 1
    pecking bird, 127
    Quaker paddle-arm, 12
    Yankee Army signalman, 25
whittling, 32-33, 183, 185
windmill
    American development of, vi-vii
    clown on bike, 64
    dovecote tinkle-turn, 115
    drum-beating, 39

    Dutch, weathervane and, 75
    fisherman, 152
    history of, iv-vi
    mad manikins pop-up, 101
    man starting automobile, 86
    merry-go-round, 139
    noise-making, 165
    spooky Indian vibrating, 165
    tubular bell, 52
working models, 157

Y

Yankee Army signalman whirligig, 25